Slightly Foxed Editions

COUNTRY BOY

SLIGHTLY FOXED EDITIONS

No. 22

COUNTRY BOY

Richard Hillyer

First published by Hodder & Stoughton in 1966

First published by Slightly Foxed in 2013
in a limited edition of 2,000 copies
of which this is copy No.

1428

Slightly Foxed Ltd
53 Hoxton Square,
London N1 6PB

A CIP catalogue record for this book is available from the British Library.

ISBN 978-1-906562-51-9

Printed by Smith Settle, Yeadon, West Yorkshire

Preface

It's human nature perhaps to look back on our early years as a time of enchantment. Kenneth Grahame, Angela Thirkell and Laurie Lee, among others, have all attempted to recapture the 'golden age' of their childhood.

My own golden age was spent in a picturesque village on the banks of the River Dart. Most villagers then were from old Devon families of farmers and fishermen whose ancestors' gravestones in the churchyard stood witness to their antiquity. The oldest church chorister and chief bell-ringer had been singing and ringing there since Victorian times. Over surrounding hillsides, horse-drawn ploughs turned green fields into patches of deep red earth each September, and along the lanes at evening the ploughman still did 'homeward plod his weary way'.

Time lends such memories a nostalgic glow, but few have recalled that now distant rural way of life with such riveting honesty as Richard Hillyer in this memoir. Richard Hillyer was the pseudonym used by Charles James Stranks, the son of a poor farm labourer, born at the dawn of the last century in the isolated Buckinghamshire village of Hardwick (here called Byfield). It was a village unchanged since Saxon times, where work was governed by the 'immemorial rhythm' of the seasons and social life revolved mostly around church and chapel and cricket pitch. It was an essentially feudal world in which the lives of the poor were dictated by the various local gentry.

Hillyer sets out to recapture a way of life which, after the Great War, had begun to disappear and was gradually fading from memory. However, his aim is more than that of mere fond recall. He wants to rescue the old English village from those who, like Hardy, offered a middle-class intellectual view of rural life, and romanticists who saw the countryside either as a place of quaint customs and ancient ways or a 'cesspit of strange iniquities peopled . . . with sadists and psychopaths'. He portrays with unflinching reality the squalor and misery of village life before the First World War, where impoverished labourers were often at the mercy of cruel and heartless farmers. Yet though his writing is unsentimental it is also wonderfully poetic, for he recaptures the magic of that remote countryside, and the effect it had on the imagination of a sensitive and highly intelligent boy with few outlets for his feelings and no one to share his interests.

For Hillyer, the impoverished labourers among whom he grew up, descendants of the old English peasantry, are the real creators of the village's character and guardians of its traditions, and it is their powers of endurance, 'courage, wisdom and sly humour' which have enabled them to survive. In old Byfield, the social order is unchangeable – everyone knows his or her place and all leave this life no better off than when they entered it. Above the Hillyers stand the Rector Mr Driffield, the Minister of the chapel Mr Bilbee, and the schoolmaster Mr Wickens, while on the very top of the heap sits the wealthy owner of Byfield House, Mr du Cane, and the Squire, Lord Postern, to whom all are expected to defer.

> [Lord Postern] would call at a cottage or two . . . not getting off his horse, but thumping with his hunting crop on the door . . . until somebody came out. Generally it was a woman . . . and she would stand in the doorway with her hands respectfully hidden under her apron, hardly daring to answer his questions with more than a plain, 'Yes, my Lord,' or 'No, my Lord.' 'Tell your husband his potatoes are looking well.' 'Yes, my Lord.' 'These your children?' nodding toward any that might have followed their mother to the door, wide-eyed and curious to see what was happening. 'Yes, my Lord.' 'Well good day to you, good day.' A touch with the crop, and the mare would move on to another.

At the very bottom lies the wretched figure of the reclusive outcast Barky Britnell, exploited and terrorized since childhood by cruel local farmers and taunted by wanton village boys.

> When [Barky] flew into one of his rages he just made hoarse, strangled sounds like a tormented animal. Some lout, who had worked him up and was enjoying the fun, showing off before other grinning louts one day, said, 'He is like a dog. Listen to him barking. Barky Britnell!' And so Barky he was.

Poor Barky's cabin is squalid beyond belief. 'A one-storeyed hut' lit by three small windows, with no fire-grate and peeling walls 'showing the yellow clay underneath festering like a sore'.

But life in Hillyer's Byfield is not all wretchedness. Blazing summer days for the children mean bathing in the village pond, and Richard recalls

> the full, rich, sensual pleasure of lying naked on the short grass, until the skin was dry, and prickly with heat, and then to plunge down into the quiet depths of the pool, among the long, smooth water-lily roots that caressed the body in passing like delicate fingers.

And there is the annual flower show in the Rectory garden, with fruit and vegetable competitions, where everybody turns out in their Sunday best for the judging, and there is dancing on the lawn to a band hired by the Rector.

Richard's immediate family – father, mother and brother John – exist on 15 shillings a week, so for them life is frugal in the extreme. In the evening, the children's supper consists of two slices of bread and dripping and a cup of cold water. Their future looks bleak. Richard, as the son of a poor labourer, can expect little more than a life crushed beneath 'the suffocating weight of endless toil'.

But this is a story of metamorphosis, of success against the heaviest odds. Richard is a bright, attentive schoolboy eager to learn. From passages of Ben Jonson, Tennyson, Dickens and the Bible which are randomly handed out in class, he discovers the magic of language that opens doors to worlds unimagined. Soon he is reading any book he can find, and Mr Wickens hints at a place at the grammar school. But hopes raised are quickly dashed. His parents could never afford the fees.

Even so, his hunger for learning remains insatiable. Salvaging an old copy of Scott's *Waverley* discarded for burning he starts a library, and the discovery of a second-hand bookstall in Billington, the nearby market town, adds poetry and classics to his collection. Then, when a prosperous uncle from Canada dies, there is hope of an inheritance which will both alleviate the family's poverty and help Richard to the grammar school. But everything goes to Mr Hillyer's sister, and the disappointment is unbearable.

So Richard is sent to work on a local farm and arrives just in time for haymaking.

> When the mowing stopped, and the horses were turned out to graze, everybody set to work to turn over yesterday's cutting. Men and boys moved in a line, each a step or two behind the other, backwards and forwards across the field at a quick walk, turning the swathe, with a deft touch of the rake, in an unbroken ribbon. It was hard to keep up at first, but as the knack grew and the movements became familiar, there was something soothing in it. All day there were the changing scents of the hayfield. The raw smell of the fresh grass in the morning, the honey smell of clover, the earthy dampness of the underside as the rakes exposed the long lines of drying grass to the sun, the sweet, dry perfume of the hay that was loaded in the evening; all of it unique, primeval, satisfying. There was the pleasure of working in company, the gossip as the haymakers moved across the field at the pace set by the leader.

It was tough, backbreaking work, yet 'I was happy in a new experience,' he writes, 'something had been added to the delight of life.' In the same way the writer in him glories in the silence of the dawn as he makes his way towards the farm to do the milking:

> There has been rain in the night, and the last leaves that still cling to the bushes hang wet and dejected. It is just growing light enough to see that they are there, the stars seem withdrawing further and further away . . . In front of me the path, without footsteps to mark it since the rain fell, looks bright and new; even the muddy places have been flattened out, and catch what light there is on their wet surfaces. For the five minutes that it takes to walk to work I am alone, in a friendly world.

For Richard the life of learning now seems to be well out of reach, but he is not discouraged. From old schoolbooks he begins to teach himself Latin, and he so astonishes the Rector with his knowledge that he is offered coaching and the prospect of sitting for a scholarship to Durham University.

Meanwhile Byfield is undergoing change. Lloyd George's old age pension brings hope to poor parishioners, and 'The Kaiser's War' further disturbs the settled order. Richard's brother John and the local farm-horses depart for France, villagers are directed into factory work, and soldiers from the industrial north are stationed in Byfield.

Then there are portents of a new, less leisurely age. The horse-drawn van, which once trundled the road to Billington slowly enough for passengers to study wildlife along the hedges, is replaced by an old gas-fuelled London bus which rattles along at speed. In a new age of travel, the old Byfield which 'imprisoned and consumed its own children' will slowly disappear.

Richard Hillyer recaptures the lost world of an old English village with realism and compassion. He depicts the villagers of Byfield with the caring eye of a Zola or a Van Gogh, lost souls resurrected – the lowly ploughman, the wretched outcast, the village schoolmaster, the pedlar, the women worn down by hopeless poverty. Hillyer is their camera, their quiet observer.

Eventually, thanks to the Rector, young Richard does manage to escape, winning a scholarship to Durham University. From the minute he first sees the city, with its great cathedral – 'that wonder among buildings' – rising above the winding medieval streets, Durham seems to have been his spiritual home. It represented everything he had longed for, cultivation and refinement and the rich life of the mind from which he had so long been excluded. When he receives the news of his scholarship we, like him, can hardly believe he has done it, the odds stacked against him were so great.

Searches have revealed little about the later life of this fascinating man, apart from the fact that he wrote a good many books, mainly on ecclesiastical subjects, and became a canon of Durham Cathedral. But in his youth we come to know him intimately. There can be few more painfully honest and moving accounts of growing up poor than *Country Boy.* It is not only a fine piece of social history, but a cliffhanger that keeps one gripped right to the end.

GORDON BOWKER

To E.L.S.

Introduction

There are some memories which, if they are to be recaptured at all, must be recaptured soon or the shape of them will be lost for ever. Among these rapidly fading things is the recollection of the life and atmosphere of remote south-country villages half a century ago, before the nineteen-fourteen war. Many people have written about the country but they have mainly concerned themselves with the squires and parsons, the farmers and small tradesmen, and let the hired labourers who made up the greater part of the community go unregarded. Yet often they were the real people of the village, the keepers of its traditions, the makers of its character: their forbears had lived there from time immemorial and generation after generation of them were recorded in the church registers. But of all the English working classes farm labourers have been the most neglected. Even Thomas Hardy for all his insight and tragic sense, looking at life from the stand-point of a middle-class intellectual, found the characters that interested him most among those who had some small stake in the community. Other writers concerned themselves mainly with quaint customs and ancient ways. Still another school, anxious to persuade the world that every village is a cesspit of strange iniquities, peopled those places with sadists and psycopaths, introducing a fey heroine of unusual beauty and sensitivity as a contrast. Perhaps, before it was possible to have much understanding of the farm labourer as a person, it was necessary to belong to his close and secretive community, to grow up with him, to feel the same pressures as he did and see his life from the underside. Because he belonged in this way, that troubled genius John Clare reflects it all better than anybody else. Living as he did at a time when the enclosure acts of the late eighteenth century were turning the English peasant into a mere hired man without rights and without friends he mirrors, both in his poetry and his autobiography, the mixture of hopelessness, patience and despair, the integrity, the few but deeply savoured pleasures of the ordinary villager. His patience was monumental, his ignorance of what went on outside his own narrow sphere profound, his life incredibly hard with no respite from the most burdensome of toil and yet he managed, amazingly, to survive as a person, often with dignity, with courage, wisdom and a sly humour which might have astonished supercilious observers if they had penetrated beneath the dulled exterior.

Change has passed over the countryside as it has over everything else, good and bad have been swept away together. So it seemed to me that it might be worth while attempting to describe that life as I saw it, growing up in the early years of this century, living in it and belonging to it. The memory has come back gladly. There may have been hardships that I have forgotten, cruelties perhaps took place that I never knew, and yet I think that the picture as a whole is a fair one. When I look back beyond the people involved to their setting, I see them wrapped in a now unbelievable quiet. In that pre-nineteen-fourteen countryside work went on in its time-honoured way without noise and without fuss. Machines were of the crudest kind. Strangers were few. The occasional tramp plodding along the gritty road, or asleep under a tall hedge, a cart or a carriage now and then, or a horseman trotting along the grass verge were the most that was to be seen. But none of the more respectable people were going far, only the tramp edging his way from casual ward to casual ward or the chance group of gypsies had their eyes on the distance. All traffic of importance had long ago deserted the roads for the rail, though the first sign of something different was just appearing as a rare motor-car passed along what was still called the turnpike in a cloud of dust. The bylanes were overgrown with grass, except where the passage of infrequent farm carts wore the herbage down a little. You could walk along them on a summer day and know that over mile after mile of meadowland and small streams not a dozen people were stirring, but the animals, the birds and the insects possessed it all. Out of that quiet world, which has now gone for ever, the people and events of this book have been recalled.

RICHARD HILLYER

Chapter 1

My grandmother, after wrestling with bitter poverty and the heartbreak that comes with it all her life, by one determined effort of will ended both. She formed her own estimate of herself – she announced that she was a lady – and from that moment behaved as such. She gave up washing, and scrubbing, and patching old, over-patched clothes, and drudging about for her family, and instead walked in the fields, when it was fine, and picked flowers to arrange, when she got home, in an old brown stewpot that stood upon the window-ledge, or strolled sedately about the lanes. On wet days she sat in the church porch, in simple dignity. It was her drawing-room, her place of state. She wore her Sunday bonnet every day, and the cross-over shawl, which she had knitted years before from many coloured wools, and kept for great occasions, was about her shoulders continually.

She was a gentle soul, and made no demands upon others for special consideration. She merely decided that she was a lady and, as far as it was in her power, lived up to that decision. At mealtimes she ate the bread and dripping, or potatoes and fat pork, that everybody else had without complaint, but ate it apart, alone. Grandfather let her go her own way. She was aware of his presence, as a duchess might have been aware of the presence of a faithful servitor, but never allowed him to intrude into her life. She had as much right to the status she had chosen as any one of the multitude of other women who were enjoying it. Her only fault was that she had not the money to go with it, to prove that she was right.

As it was, the neighbours began to talk. They said that Sally Hillyer was mad. Better-class people, who were offended by Granny's claims which seemed to cast a slight on their own, said that she had delusions of grandeur. They were quite wrong. Her act of will was sincere. She had no delusions. The soul-corroding poverty, which she shut out of her life, was the illusion now. Penury and wealth no longer existed. She took her stand on her own, natural worth as sufficient support for her dignity. But the neighbours began to talk. The Rector came on a special visit, and then sent the doctor. Between them they shut her up in the County Asylum. Grandfather would have kept her at home if he could. She did no harm, and was in nobody's way, but they did not let him have much say in the matter. When she went he lost heart, and it wasn't very long before he died.

So all the rest of Granny's waking existence was spent sitting in a scrubbed wooden armchair, with twenty or thirty other old women, each with her own particular rebellion against the world, sitting in similar chairs, arranged round the bare, whitewashed walls of a bleak room in a place like a prison. The sole interest in the future still left to these yellow old shells of people was, which of the nodding bundles by the fire would die next, so that the rest could move up a place nearer the blaze. The draughty spots by the door were good enough for newcomers. There they sat, folding and unfolding their skinny hands, distorted by a lifetime of hard work and crippling rheumatism; helpless, hopeless, beaten. All except Grandmother. She remained aloof, shutting herself up in the fortress of her ladyship and ignoring the common world.

That is how I remember her, when the confused impression remaining from the three or four visits I made with Mother clears itself a little. There is a thin, pale-faced little creature with a bonnet and a cross-over shawl on, sitting huddled in a chair among the rest; with the smell of stale bread, and scrubbing, and mad people all about that grim place. I never recollect her speaking to me, she would just nod, and smile, as if that was all I could expect. But I remember her funeral very vividly. She had three children, but Father was the only one within reach so he was told to fetch away the body. He borrowed a spring cart and brought her home, in the dusk of a showery evening, with the feet end of the coffin sticking out over the tail-board, and the head of it between his legs. A piece of black cloth, that did not quite cover the unpainted wood, had been thrown over the protruding part to hide it a little, as a mark of respect. It was the best he could do. We only had one living-room in our house, so the coffin stood there, with the lid pushed back, and the still face, lying fringed with an old-fashioned nightcap, for all to see. One by one the neighbours dropped in to look at her and chat a bit, while Father and Mother sat in their armchairs, by the fire, with the dignity of people who had something of great consequence in their keeping. Death was strange to me but not frightening, just clean, solemn and very important.

The churchyard was not above a quarter of a mile away, and we walked there in a little procession, with four men at the head of us pushing the old black bier that Byfield people had used for hundreds of years at village funerals. On the coffin lay a bunch of primroses out of our garden, and some late daffodils. There had been a high wind the night before, and the road was thick with broken twigs, which carried small, bright, green leaves just bursting from their outworn bud-cases, as if they had been strewn there for us to walk on. The wind was still gusty, chasing broken bits of cloud across the sky and interfering with the sound of the mourning bell. Sometimes its slow note fell round and heavy, like a ball of lead dropping into still water, sometimes tossed and frayed as the wind caught it. Up in the trees alongside the lane, where the branches were already misty green, the rooks were busy putting their nests in order, with a good deal of agitated flapping about as the branches tossed beneath them. A unity ran through everything, binding it into one thought, one impression. It was all a part of Granny's funeral.

Just inside the churchyard, standing well back from the path so as not to be in our way, were half a dozen or so of Granny's friends. Old women, with their hands folded in front of them and wrapped in the ends of their shawls, their heads nodding in gentle emphasis of the talk that was going on, quietly, among them. It would not have been good manners to intrude on the family, but they had known Sally since she was a girl, and understood her troubles, which were like their own. So they had come to pay their respects when she was put into the earth, and to enjoy the unaccustomed stir of a funeral.

There was nothing that seemed to me sad about what we

were doing, it was all quite natural, but very important. The familiar sound of the Rector's voice seemed just that much different in the open air, when he began, 'I am the resurrection and the life.' Awareness awoke in me, a sensitiveness to moods, and people, and places, which has come back to me many times since, enlarging life and bringing both pleasure and pain beyond my proper share. Every sight and sound throbbed with a vitality of its own, and cried to me like a living thing.

The unvarnished coffin, with its primroses and daffodils, went down between the smooth, wet walls of the grave, whose surfaces had been trimmed and tidied by the grave-digger and still showed the grooves cut by his spade, like chisel marks on wood. Everything to do with the dead was done carefully. As soon as you get down a little our land is heavy yellow clay, so the clods we threw in when the Rector said, 'ashes to ashes and dust to dust', fell with a thump on the coffin. It was all over, and we stood back to let everybody who was in the churchyard come and look in the grave, and read how old she was, and perhaps drop in a flower or two if they had any. The Rector shook hands with my father and walked off, holding up his cassock, and picking his way with his shiny boots through the wet grass. Johnny Batson put the bier back in the belfrey, where it belonged, and we went home. All our importance had disappeared. We were not people with a funeral any more.

Chapter 2

Our house was in Brandy Hole Lane. Old people said it was called that because a public house had stood there once, called the Brandy Hole, but there was no sign of it now, and nobody quite knew where it had been. Just at the curve in the lane, where the road from the church bent round to go up into the village, was a low, thatched cottage standing back in a bit of garden. The weather-beaten, ancient brickwork bulged in places out of the half-rotten timber frame that intersected it. The place was very old. Perhaps it was a piece of building that had belonged to the Brandy Hole itself once, though its past was forgotten. It had certainly been larger at one time, but now there was only one room up and another down, with a sort of brick barn stuck on at one end. That was the house where we lived. It was the first place that I was conscious of. The shell from which I emerged. The world in microcosm. All other houses, all other belongings, were judged by our house and our belongings. Four of us lived there. Mother, Father, John and myself.

When you went in you found that the door did not open directly into the living-room, as it did in most of the village houses, but into a little dark entry place, out of which some warped old stairs climbed steeply to the upper storey. Getting into the house was something of a manoeuvre. First you stepped into the little lobby, and closed the outer door, otherwise it blocked the one you had to open to get into the living-room. If you were unfamiliar with the place, you might have to fumble round in the dark quite a bit, to find the latch of the inner door. When you got that open, you were in a fair-sized living-room, floored with ordinary wall bricks, which Mother kept scrubbed to a deep, clean red. The low ceiling of the place was crossed with brown oak beams, about two feet apart; the space between them was painted white. It used to be covered all over with whitewash, coat after coat of it until it was about half an inch thick, until Lord Postern, who was our landlord and charged us eighteen pence a week, was allowed by his agent to come in one day and look round. There were not many cottages where he was let do that, but Mother had a reputation for keeping everything spotlessly clean, so we were one of the agent's show places. His Lordship noticed the old beams, hidden away under all that whitewash, and took a fancy to have them scraped and painted. It was a dusty job and took days to do, we had to live outside while the man was at it; but Mother was pleased, and it gave us distinction in the village to have such a ceiling.

Until Ellen, my sister, was about thirteen we all slept in one room upstairs, then Mother said she wouldn't stand it any more. It wasn't right for a big girl to be growing up like that. She'd have another room or know the reason why. The barn could be built up a bit higher and have a bedroom put on top of it. So, from then on, whenever Lord Postern's agent was in the village, she went after him about it. But she never got any satisfaction. He always said, 'I see your point, Mrs Hillyer. We shall have to think about it,' and then rode off, or started talking to somebody else, but never did anything. She got pretty well desperate in the end, and when she got desperate there was no stopping her. She made Father take time off from work, between milking and milking, say from ten in the morning till three in the afternoon. It needed something pretty serious to justify doing that. He was to go over to Billington, where the agent's office was, and not come back until he had got the other bedroom. She would have been the better one to go, we all knew that, Father as much as anybody else, but it wouldn't have looked right. It wasn't a woman's place to do that sort of thing. He wouldn't have much time, but he could just about do it if he walked across the fields instead of going by the road, and he could take a bit of dinner in his pocket and eat it as he went along. So he washed and shaved, and put on a clean pair of trousers and a tidy jacket; not his Sunday clothes, that wouldn't have looked right either for a working man, on a weekday, and the agent wouldn't have liked it if he had gone all dressed up. Before he went Mother drilled him in what he was to say, and made him vow he would say it.

He set off like a man going to the stake, but confident in the higher purpose that sent him there. He came back triumphant. The agent had told him that he could get Billy Makins, who did odd jobs about the estate, to build us the bedroom. To the end of his life the tale of that day's doings was Father's proudest saga. How he sat waiting for over an hour in a little office, watching a clerk writing, until the agent said that he would see him. What the agent had said to him, and what he had said to the agent, and how, at last, when it was getting on for one o'clock, and the agent was putting on his hat and coat, and it looked as if you could no more bend him than you could a cast-iron man, the agent had suddenly said, 'Damn it all! Get Billy Makins to put one up then, and perhaps you'll be satisfied.' Father always thought that this triumph was due to his pertinacity, to the strength of the arguments Mother had supplied him with, to his skill as a negotiator, but there was a general election coming up at the time, and perhaps that had something to do with it. A rash man was putting up as a Liberal against Lord Postern's Tory candidate, and he was said to be writing pieces in the London papers about the scandalous state of farm labourers' cottages.

But whatever the cause we got our bedroom. Ellen went away to service just then, and Mother bought an old, wooden double bed from somewhere, which just about filled up the room, with no more than a foot or two all round it to move about in, and John and I had it between us. Where it had started life nobody knew, but it had been a good one in its day. Its colour was pale green, with a basket of roses painted on the headboard, and another at the foot, and there was a thin spray of flowers climbing up each of the posts. Two thick palliasses filled the wooden frame, and with a flock bed on the top of them it was warm and comfortable. There were two texts pinned up on the walls. They were something to look at when you were dropping off to sleep. One said, 'Thy word is a lantern unto my feet, and a light unto my paths.' That was a good one. Ellen had written it out herself in red ink and drawn a lantern at the top, with a path that went all round the edges and led up to the lantern again. She had put people, and flowers, and rabbits, and things like that on the path. Ellen was good at drawing. The other text said, 'My times are in Thy hand,' and was only printed.

Lord Postern himself came to look at our new bedroom, when Billy Makins had finished it. He generally rode round the estate once a year or so, particularly at election times, with a groom behind him. He would come trotting into the village on his bay mare, wearing one of those roundish hats that are halfway between a top hat and a bowler. He looked almost like an ordinary person in his tweed coat and breeches, with cloth gaiters instead of top-boots. He would call at a cottage or two and be affable, not getting off his horse but thumping with his hunting crop on the door, or the palings, whichever was handiest, until somebody came out. Generally it was a woman – the men were all at work – and she would stand in the doorway with her hands respectfully hidden under her apron, hardly daring to answer his questions with more than a plain 'Yes, my Lord' or 'No, my Lord'. 'Tell your husband his potatoes are looking well.' 'Yes, my Lord.' 'These your children?' nodding toward any that might have followed their mother to the door, wide-eyed and curious to see what was happening. 'Yes, my Lord.' 'Well good day to you, good day.' A touch with the crop, and the mare would move on to another selected cottage, where the catechism would be gone through again, changing potatoes to flowers, or greens, or whatever might be in sight, and children to cat, or dog, or chickens as the circumstances required.

When the word went round that his Lordship was here, Mr Wickens, our schoolmaster, would stop lessons and tell us to straighten up our hair and button our jackets, and line us up by the school-yard wall, and tell us to stop scuffling about with our feet and behave respectfully for once. All the boys were bareheaded but this being a ceremonial occasion Mr Wickens wore his bowler hat. Where we stood, facing the green, we could not see the road his Lordship would come along; but at the sound of a couple of horses trotting up past the Pheasant, which was just round the bend to the right of us, Mr Wickens took off his bowler, and awe descended upon us. They are pulling up in front of us almost as soon as they come in sight, first his Lordship, then William the groom, a yard or two behind him. His Lordship affects to look surprised. 'What's this? What's this? Not in school at this time of day! Oh, I see. Let out specially,' and he nods towards Mr Wickens, who is standing, hat in hand, to one side of us. 'William, give them all a penny.' William, knowing the routine, gets stiffly down from his horse. An old wound in the knee, got while he was with his Lordship in the Yeomanry fighting the Boers, still troubles him a bit. He scoops a handful of coppers from his breeches' pocket, and limps along the line, putting a penny into each outstretched hand while we murmur our thanks, hardly knowing whether to direct them to William, who actually bestows the gift, or to its provider, sitting impatiently on his horse while the groom plods along the line.

Occasionally a tenant of one of his Lordship's cottages, more than usually desperate for some long overdue repair or primitive amenity, would come and try to put her case while this was going on, her voice shrill with pumped-up courage, while his Lordship, anxious that his generosity should have the full support of his presence, was unable to get away. If she came by herself she might obtain what she wanted, or at least be promised it, for it would still have to be wrested from the agent, and that was like taking meat from a tiger, though his Lordship's word was some help. If two or three came on a similar errand he would get angry and wave them away, saying, 'See Mr Bond, see Mr Bond,' as he rose in his stirrups, gave the horse a cut with his crop, and rode off without waiting for the three cheers which were the proper conclusion to the ceremony. If that happened, Mr Wickens would be short with us as he hustled us back into school, for he had not shaken hands with his Lordship as he expected to do. Next rent day, Mr Bond, the agent, would have some sharp words to say about 'troubling his Lordship', and 'imposing on his Lordship', and the needed repairs, or alterations, or reduction in rent, would be further off than ever. It had to be well understood that visits like this were special acts of grace, and were not to be taken advantage of.

Not that they happened very frequently, once a year at most, except at election time. As the principal landowner in the district Lord Postern expected to have a big say in who was sent to Parliament. Not that he was in any way crude about it, or issued orders, or anything like that. There was nothing you could put your finger on, and show him up about, even if anybody wanted to show him up, which nobody did except a few disgruntled radicals, and who took any notice of them? But somehow or other, round election time, it would be put about that if Lord Postern did not get his friend into Parliament he would lose interest, and sell his property, and we should all be turned out, or the rents would go up, and there might not be any foxhounds, and whoever bought the property wouldn't take the interest in it which his Lordship took, and the bay mare and the round hat would make their appearance in the village with William in attendance, and perhaps a small repair or two would get done. It was even rumoured that, if it had been a wet harvest that year, the farmers got a discount on their rent, but we never knew that for certain because they were pretty close about it, in case the men should ask for a rise. All this seemed a natural accompaniment to election times, like speeches, and the promise of better days ahead for poor people, but everything quieted down when the election was over.

Gentry who came down from London for the hunting, visitors to the rectory, and people like that, said how picturesque the village was, with its tumbly, thatched-roofed cottages, and all that air of being ages old, and how sensible it was of Lord Postern to keep it like that.

Chapter 3

The little group of houses was called Byfield, at least that was its name on the map, and outsiders called it that, though people belonging to the neighbourhood generally put in another 'f', and called it Biffild. I grew up with its indelible marks upon me, so that I can never detach myself from its influence. I see myself, in those early days, responding to its stimulus, becoming a person in answer to the pressures it put upon me, developing in this direction or that by reason of the people who lived there. They were just run-of-the-mill people, as different, and separate, in their characters as run-of-the-mill people usually are, feeling the life in them and enjoying the feel of it. They were basic human nature, and, growing up along with them, you learned how extraordinary that is, and so were free for ever from the silly snobbishness of dismissing ordinary people as of no account because they have not got the particular shine on them you think fine.

The Rector called it 'The Village', and so did the people at Byfield House, and Mrs Blore. This had the effect of setting them apart, as if they lived somewhere else. The rest of us just called it home, or, if we lived on its outskirts and had to go to the centre for anything, we said we were going up town. We had two greens and that was a distinction, because most villages had only one. On the top green was the pump, and an old hollow elm tree which people were proud of as a curiosity, and there was the pond on one side, and the school on the other. On a rough piece of ground at the top end stood an old, clay-walled cottage, with a fragment of neglected garden. There had been three at one time, but two were ruined now, with their roofs fallen in and lying all askew within the broken walls, in a heap of rotten thatch and shattered rafters. Only the middle cabin was occupied, though locked and deserted all day, and, with tufts of rank grass growing on the decaying roof, it looked as dismal as the rest. People kept away from that side of the green generally.

Down at the other end of the village was the lower green. The turf was good there, and it was big enough for a cricket pitch. It was a pleasant place to be on a summer evening, when there was a game on, and the men who were not working in their gardens sat on an old, fallen tree-trunk, nursing a puff or two of tobacco in their blackened clay pipes, making occasional slow comments to each other on the game, or their work, or the weather. The old tree had come down long ago, and now lay with its bark dropped off, and the grey wood underneath polished and shiny with the friction of many generations of corduroy trousers. Away beyond Johnny Batson's apple trees, you could see the top half of the church tower, with its round-faced clock and gilt hands, shining in the evening sun. The rectory was to the right, hidden behind a high brick wall and a line of great chestnut trees.

It has just struck eight, and I am standing in the outfield waiting for the ball to come my way, but not minding much if it doesn't. I am not very good at cricket and don't like it, but I had rather be out of doors on a summer evening even if it means playing cricket, because half past seven is my bedtime, summer and winter, whether I want to go or not, and at eleven years old I am inclined to rebel. I see my mother coming round the corner by Eliza Bone's house. She is slightly built, about average height for a woman as it seems to me. She has a blue-striped cotton blouse on, with a high collar and tight sleeves. I know it well enough for I saw her make it. Her fair hair is drawn back tightly from her high forehead and twisted into a hard little bun at the back. She wears a clean white apron over an old, patched grey skirt, 'patched but tidy', as she would say. Her laced-up, black boots are old too, but well cobbled and still serviceable.

She calls sharply, 'Richard,' in her clear voice, and as I look in her direction she beckons for me to come, but I know that I needn't go just yet. Old Eliza has caught sight of her sure enough, and comes hobbling out for a gossip. Mother will do her best to cut it short; not that she dislikes old Eliza, who is a very privileged person in her way; she lays out dead people, and goes to houses when babies are born, and generally has all the news there is going, but Mother does not hold with gossiping about in the road. However, politeness will demand that she stays five minutes or so. When she calls again I shall have to go. Eliza tries to keep us, and follows us for a few yards as we edge away, hobbling along on her stick. Then Mother moves off quickly, pushing me in front of her and saying, 'It's time this boy was in bed, Mrs Bone. Bob will be home for his supper in a minute,' and I am hustled off down the lane.

It is a summer evening, and I am in good spirits, so I go ahead of her with a kind of hopping, skipping movement which I like, and always use when I am pleased with myself. Not that there is anything special to be pleased about, I am just pleased. Father has come out of the garden and stands scraping the dirt off his spade with a little bit of slate, before hanging it up on its nail beneath the eaves. He has a round, pleasant face, with a little moustache, black like his close-cropped hair. It is fascinating to watch him trimming this moustache, which he does on a Sunday morning, using Mother's scissors and a little triangle of looking-glass. Now he stands carefully scraping the spade, making an inch or so of clean, bright steel show through the clay at every movement. He is short, but strongly built, with heavy farm boots, brown cord trousers tied with a piece of string just below the knees, a blue and white striped cotton shirt, with the sleeves rolled up but no collar, showing beneath his open waistcoat; whose pockets bulge with a tin tobacco box and a short clay pipe on one side, and a five-shilling Ingersol watch with an old horse curb for a chain, on the other. In the winter time he has a leather strap round his throat, but it is bare now, brown and sinewy, with a scattering of little curly black hairs on it.

I have no kind of fear or constraint with my father. Mother is different, you never quite know. Things went on in Mother's head that were difficult to guess at. Father is always easy to understand. For him life was simple and had no worries. If he worked, and earned what money he could, Mother would see to the rest. In a dumb, speechless sort of way he loved and admired her beyond all things, and believed her capable of dealing with any crisis which might arise for any of us. Beyond that his thoughts did not go. Every Saturday night he gave her his wages, the full fifteen shillings a week he earned as a cowman at Bratton's farm, and she gave him back a shilling for himself, which he carefully put away in the old fustian bag, folded over into four, which he used as a purse. Out of that he bought half an ounce of tobacco a week, and paid for all the seeds he needed in his garden, and still contrived to save a shilling or two to spend on special occasions. The hour after supper, before going to bed, is the only time he has to himself these summer days; for all the rest, from six o'clock in the morning till now, he is either round at the farm at work, or in his garden, just snatching a minute or two for his dinner and tea. So he doesn't talk much now, he is too tired, and there isn't much to say anyway. He is just pleased with himself because he is resting.

I eat my two slices of bread and dripping with a cup of cold water, say my prayers, and get into bed. John is two years older than me, and hasn't come in yet. For a minute or two I lie awake, hoping he will come, so that I can find out what he has been doing all the evening. I stare at the wallpaper, trying to work out the pattern of blue roses that wind in and out on a yellow background. Just outside the window I can see the top of an elm tree, with the birds that live in it coming home for the night. They settle on a branch for a second or two, look as if they intend to stay there, then shuffle about a little and skip off somewhere else, and go through the business again. At last they quiet down. I watch them in a sleepy way, and the next thing is, it's morning.

The old, cracked bell on the top of the school is rattling vigorously away as I set off up the lane. There is no need to hurry, it will go on for five minutes at least, nearer ten sometimes, depending on who is ringing it. Boys take it in turns, but everybody wants to get rid of the rackety old thing and get a new one; so some of them start early, and wrench away at it enough to tear it off its pivot, but it holds on somehow. Even when it stops there will be another minute or two, while the children form up in the school yard and wait for the master to come out of his house, and march them in to begin lessons.

Mr Wickens, our schoolmaster, was a tall, thin man, though at first he didn't strike you as tall because he stooped a good deal, as if he hadn't strength enough to hold himself upright. But he had a way of jerking his head back now and again, and pulling himself up, and then you saw how tall he really was. He had a thin, pointed beard and a straggling moustache which he was always brushing to one side or the other with a folded white handkerchief. He and his wife, a bony, ginger-haired woman with a whining voice, ran the school. Mr Wickens was an important man. He drew up wills for those people who had anything to leave, and measured land, and was secretary of practically everything in the village that needed a secretary; like the Flower Show Committee, and the Parish Council, and the trustees of Dr Randall's Charity. Working people didn't altogether trust him. He was too much under the thumb of the farmers. When he measured land at harvest time, and settled just how much each man had cut, so that he could draw his money for it at piece-work rates, they were pretty sure that he made it less than it was, so that he could save the farmer's pockets. He was a prim man, with a prim conscience, and would not have done anything like that for the world, but he only had himself to thank for people saying that he would; because the way in which he spoke to the farmers made you sure that he would give way to them in everything, and nobody had any doubts about them robbing the men if they could.

Mr Wickens was really a bit of a puzzle. He was well above the ordinary run of village schoolmasters, but he did not seem to make any effort to move to anything better, though he was not contented. He just stayed on and lived with his disappointments. Whatever it was that he hoped for had not come, and he was not the sort of man to make fortune favour him. Every year that he stayed on in Byfield the less likely he was to leave, and the more his grumbling sounded as if he never expected to do anything about it. 'Yes,' he would say, 'I plod along. I plod along. There really is so little encouragement. No scope at all. The boys all go to work on the farms, and the girls to domestic service. There is nothing to be done with them, nothing at all.' So he had given up looking for children bright enough to take trouble over. He did not think that there were any. But what he had to teach he taught well, because he was a born teacher. His greatest interest was his bicycle, which was one of the few in the village. He had even invented a new sort of saddle for it, made out of string-netting with little rubber pads in the proper places. It was going to make his fortune, when he had interested the right people. He was always explaining how much more comfortable it was than the ordinary leather ones, and pointing out that it could not make you hot, because it was adequately ventilated, or turn trouser seats thin and shiny, which were great advantages. Every summer he went off on it for a week's holiday, and was said to have got as far away as Norfolk once or twice. When he got back he used to make little alterations in his invention, so perhaps he never got it perfect enough to show to the bicycle makers. But we were lucky to have him. He was well above the ordinary run of village schoolmasters.

There was a mystery about him that we never got to the bottom of. Every now and then, he would come quickly out of school at the end of morning lessons, with his bowler hat and trouser clips on, get his bicycle out of the tool shed, and set off towards Billington at a good pace, for him. What he did when he got there we never found out, but whatever it was it can't have taken him long, because he had to make the five miles there and back and do whatever it was in about an hour, but he always managed it. He used to come puffing up, just as the afternoon school bell was ringing; and we always started it a minute or two early, but we could never catch him out however much we tried. I expect most schoolmasters would have set us to work, and then slipped indoors for some dinner, after a rush like that, but not Mr Wickens. He wouldn't eat in front of his class either, that would have been unprofessional. So he had a plate of sandwiches, and a glass of milk, on the window ledge in the lobby. During the first half hour of school he would be popping in and out all the time, getting a bite of sandwich, and a gulp of milk, among the hats and coats in the brown, glazed-brick lobby.

He used to try and make it seem as if he was going somewhere else but always came back looking guilty, and brushing his sandy moustache with a folded handkerchief in his usual way. It might take him half a dozen trips of that sort before he got through his milk and sandwiches. We were not supposed to know what was going on, but we knew all about it right enough. It was easy for the boy who sat next to the door to slip out for a second, while Mr Wickens's back was turned, and if he was pretty quick he could count the sandwiches, and find out what was in them. Then, when he was in his place again, and Wickens was looking the other way, he would pull his face into a shape as if he was saying, 'Five, cheese and lettuce', or 'Four, ham and beetroot', or whatever it was, so we always knew. But with the curious courtesy of boys for those they like, we never let on that we knew, or spoiled his little deception in any way.

Lessons dragged along as a rule. They were easy enough to learn, but nobody wanted to bother, what was the good of it anyway? Wickens had given up trying, though once a week he did make the school come alive. At precisely half past three, on a Wednesday afternoon, he would put away the book he was using, slapping down the lid of his tall, wobbly-legged desk as if he was glad to see the back of it, and unpin an exercise book that was fastened up by the door. He would carry it back to his desk, flatten it out, because hanging up all the week used to make it curl up a lot, lodge his pince-nez on to his nose and say, in a tone that suggested he was interested for once, 'Well, let's see what the combined intelligence of the class has produced for us this week.' Everybody sat up and listened. This was where Mr Know-all was going to get caught out. 'What's this? I fear some boy has been misusing this book. I will not try and find out who it is, but if it occurs again I shall know whom to punish.' Some idiot had tried to slip in something funny, without signing his name, but what was the good of that when Wickens knew everybody's handwriting? 'Ah, this is better. What is a poet laureate?' I had put that one in, because I had read in *Lloyd's Weekly News*, the paper we took at home, something about a poet laureate, and it sounded interesting. I really wanted to know.

So, for ten minutes, he let himself go on it, and education began for me. There was Ben Jonson, the butt of canary wine, birthday odes and all the rest of it. I was fascinated. My mind was being broken out of its shell. Here were wonderful things to know. Things that went beyond the small utilities of our lives, which was all that school had seemed to concern itself with until then. Knowledge of this sort could make all times, and places, your own. You could be anybody, and everybody, and still be yourself all the time. If the thoughts did not shape themselves as clearly as this, that was the sense of what lay behind the excitement of listening to Wickens at that moment. He dropped the subject, not very willingly as it seemed, for the interest went out of his voice as he passed on to the usual run of questions. 'What makes cart wheels squeak when they aren't greased?' 'What makes shooting stars?' 'Why can fish live in water?' and many of the other mysteries of day-to-day existence. It was the passion of every boy's life to catch Wickens out on one or other of these things, rather than real curiosity, that lay behind all this diverse enquiry. The schoolmaster knew that well enough, yet something in him made him go on doing it. He must have hoped that it was worth while, that closed minds were being opened a little, that children who might have gone through life incurious as the dumbest animals were being taught to notice, and ask questions, and that it would tell some day perhaps.

The question about poets laureate linked up with something else that Mr Wickens started about that time. From somewhere or other he had collected about a couple of dozen books, which were not just lesson books. They were an odd lot. Some were complete, others only selections, a chapter or two from some classic which a careful editor had thought suitable for children to read, but there was something in them all. Among them were a few poems of Tennyson, printed on brittle, brownish paper, with a gaudy cover. It said on the title page that he was 'Poet Laureate' and that set me wanting to read them. The coloured words flashed out and entranced my fancy. They drew pictures in the mind. Words became magical, incantations, abracadabra which called up spirits. My dormant imagination opened like a flower in the sun. Life at home was drab and colourless, with nothing to light up the dull monotony of the unchanging days. Here in books was a limitless world that I could have for my own. It was like coming up from the bottom of the ocean and seeing the universe for the first time.

So this Friday half hour shone over all the week. When the books were given out we were left to ourselves. The only rule was that we should stick to the book we chose until we had read it, and not swap about. So, for one swiftly passing thirty minutes, I could be with Captain Dodd, brave yet anxious, as that ominous schooner, lateen-rigged, which was no doubt something tremendous in the way of rigging, slipped out from behind the island, its ports open, the guns run out, as the villainous crew flashed their cutlasses on deck or grouped round the carronade, a mass of dark faces with a glint of gold about their ears. I had a good ship, and a brave crew, but there were ladies on board, and in that portentous pocket-book, which lay just above my heart, were the anxiously won savings, the *Hard Cash*, which I was carrying home to my family through so many perils. How many more perils there were to come I did not know for years, as the book was only an extract, hardly more than the one chapter with that famous sea fight, but I stood on the bridge at the end of it sorely wounded but triumphant, and yelled at the crippled pirate, 'Goodbye ye Portuguese lubber, outmanoeuvred, outfought and outsailed.' Could anything be more satisfactory to throw at a beaten enemy than that magnificent mouthful?

Black Beauty was a favourite, though I didn't think much of horses in real life, so was *Treasure Island.* I met Sam Weller first on one of those Friday afternoons, and got into trouble for laughing out loud. And there was *Masterman Ready*, and the *Three Midshipmen*, and curiously enough *Cranford,* which nobody wanted very much because it was only about a village like our own. The half hour was gone almost before the book was opened, and that miserable bell on Wickens's desk, with its silly ping, ping, meant that we had got to stop, and hand in whatever we were reading. But the dream would linger if you encouraged it, perhaps for an hour or two, until the heavy reality of life encroached once more, and pushed it into the back of the mind.

Books came to me like a new sense but they were hard to get hold of. Mother had a few, Sunday School prizes mostly, though there were two that she got when she was up at Byfield House helping with the spring cleaning once, that I looked into but couldn't make much of. They were called *Miriam's Schooling* and *The Revolution in Tanner's Lane*, by a man called Mark Rutherford. They seemed harsh and gloomy to me, but Mother liked them, and read them quite a lot. Here and there, about the village, a book or two could be found and these I borrowed. I got hold of most of Dickens in that way, in knocked-about old copies that had been picked up at a rummage sale for a penny, or thrown in with a heap of odds and ends to make a bargain for sixpence. The Bible was one of our school books. Nobody complained about that, because if you liked books at all the Bible was as exciting as any, it was so full of turbulence and strangeness. You could feel the heat of the desert, and hear the camel bells, as the caravans passed over the wild roads to ancient cities. And the people were so much larger than the people in other books, filled with more urgent desires, so grand and yet so simple. There was Abraham, wandering with his tent and flocks and herds through the timeless past in search of the future. David and Jonathan, bound in that deathless friendship. Saul, mad and broken, leaning on his spear and waiting for the welcome stroke that would end his shame. Above all there was David, old and tired, sick of kingship and its troubles, hearing of the death of the evil son he loved so greatly, and turning to seek a hiding place for the grief he could not contain, 'O my son Absalom, my son, my son Absalom! Would God I had died for thee, O Absalom, my son, my son!' Words like that did things to me. It seemed as if my heart would break with David's.

There was the excitement of words too in the Church Catechism – the run and rhythm of it. 'To keep my hands from picking and stealing, and my tongue from evil speaking, lying, slandering.' It did not matter what it was about, the swing of the sound was itself perfectly satisfying, and yet the heavy fall at the end of the sentence made lying and slandering seem the most odious of crimes. 'To learn and labour truly to get mine own living' had a sort of honest ring about it that was pleasing. 'And to do my duty in that state of life unto which it shall please God to call me.' That hinted at possibilities ahead, but it was not easy to see what they were.

Chapter 4

Lord Postern, and religion, entered the consciousness of every child as soon as he knew anything more than how to eat and drink and walk about. Lord Postern was the ultimate earthly influence. He owned the houses we lived in. In an indirect way, through the farmers, he settled how everybody was to work, and what they were to get for it; because if times were hard, and his Lordship did not reduce the rents, farmers got rid of some of their men, or cut down wages, and there was nothing anybody could do about it because there were no other jobs to be had. He was the boundary to everybody's thinking. You couldn't go beyond his Lordship. Except of course to One Above. He was always there. Religion was the pivot on which we turned. There it was, fixed, immovable, both controlling us and encouraging us, giving us an importance we shouldn't have had without it. Religion supplied the literature, philosophy, music and drama of a population the bulk of which could barely read. It had two faces, church and chapel. Church meant the Rector, Mr Driffield, chapel meant Mr Bilbee.

Mr Driffield was a handsome old man of nearly seventy, tall and rather stout, with white hair and a fresh complexion; his black frock coat and flat, round parson's hat suited him very well. Every afternoon he was out and about, visiting all the houses in the parish in strict rotation; making no difference between church and chapel, because he thought chapel-going a rather low habit, which kindness demanded he should overlook. Every woman in the village knew the Rector's day as well as she knew the butcher's or the baker's, and would have the fireplace tidied up, her face washed, and a clean apron on before he came. If not, some courteous but unmistakable hint would show that he had noticed the slackness. Where there was any particular need he would leave a gift behind, half-a-crown or so, laid unobtrusively on the corner of the table where he had been sitting, or put on the window-ledge as he went out. Nothing to hurt anybody's feelings. If people who were ill needed medicines, or special food, they got it from the rectory; only then it would be given out by one of his daughters. He had a lot of them, all unmarried, and they visited as regularly as he did, though they were not so stately about it.

Now and again Mrs Driffield herself would come round, but only on very fine days, because she was supposed to be rather an invalid. She always wore a black silk dress, with a gold watch pinned on the front of it, face down. The women liked her to come because, as the mother of a large family, she was supposed to understand things, and be easy to talk to, though they were sorry for her because none of her girls got married. The general opinion was that the Rector ought to have stayed in a town parish, where he could have had curates, and married some of the girls off to them. Of course nobody ever said that to Mrs Driffield, but they felt it all the same. People always talked carefully, and correctly, to her, and tried not to use ignorant country words.

Mother used to sit very stiff and upright, with her hands folded in her lap. 'I hope the Rector has got rid of his lumbago, ma'am, now that the fine weather has come.' 'Yes, Mrs Hillyer, I am glad to say that he is very well again. I hope your family are all well.' 'Yes, ma'am, thank God, we haven't any trouble of that sort in the house at present. How pretty Miss Lucy made the flowers look in church, last Sunday. I always say, that for making the best of flowers, there is nobody like Miss Lucy.' 'Yes, I suppose she is quite clever that way, she has done them for so long, you see. She always did the flowers when we were in London.' And so the stately conversation would proceed, never touching on anything at all intimate, until Mrs Driffield, turning her watch face uppermost to see the time, would say, 'Dear me, Mrs Hillyer, I have been here half an hour, how fast the time seems to go when I come to your house!' And Mother, wrestling with the inner door which always stuck a bit, would say, 'It's a pleasure to see you, ma'am. It's nice to talk to somebody who can understand. Good afternoon, ma'am.' 'Good afternoon, Mrs Hillyer.' The Rector's wife would go her way, a thought more calm, a thought more complacent, and Mother would sit down and preen herself for a minute, before going on with the afternoon's routine. Both of them had enjoyed themselves. It was as if there was some subtle understanding between them, which had been refreshed by the visit.

Occasionally the rectory had visitors, and of course the village knew all about them. The one who came most was a little, frail old man with long white hair which blew about as he walked. He was the head of the college at Oxford which gave

Mr Driffield the living, and he took a great interest in everything in the village. He used to give magic lantern talks in the schoolroom on Switzerland, and How We Got The Bible, and Great Men of History, and subjects like that. It was wonderful for a man to have all that knowledge. When he spoke it was with a quiet authority which people not only accepted but also liked to hear. It must be splendid to be a scholar, to live securely, to know about the world, and books, and people. Words are pictures really, and for me 'scholar' always meant Mr Brearley, his thin face and bent, hurrying figure, and his voice which was so beautiful to hear. I wished I could be a scholar.

The biggest sight of the week, when Mr Du Cane and his mother were at home, was to see them turn up at church on Sunday morning. People would get there early so as not to miss them and hang about, even after the bell stopped, if they were a little late, though the Rector was down on that sort of thing. You could see the carriage and pair coming up the lane. There was a sort of excitement about it. The sleek, brown horses, groomed until their coats shone, their polished hooves springing from the ground as if they were too dainty to touch it. Their tossing heads, and dark, liquid eyes, which just caught a glimpse of you out of their blinkers when the reins checked them as they pulled up and brought their heads round in your direction. The glossy patent-leather harness, with silver fittings, polished to a soft bright glow. The carriage swinging lightly from its high springs, the jet black body of it, picked out with a thin gold line here and there, and the coat of arms on the door, which shone out from the fathomless dark gloss of all the rest. The wonderful steps, which unfolded, and fell into their proper place as steps when the door opened. The passengers getting out, Mr Du Cane first, a middle-aged, red-faced man in a black frock coat and top hat; then his mother, an old lady, whom he carefully helped down the steps in a haze of shawls and lacy things. It was all a delight to look at, and a wonder in every part.

When the Byfield House people were in their seat, just in front of the lectern, the Rector started the service. He didn't begin until then even if they were a minute or two late, which they were not very often, though he did not like it. Every now and then, at the beginning of hymns and times like that, Mr Du Cane would stand up and take a good look round the church to make sure that everybody was there who ought to be. They generally were on Sunday mornings, though at night a good many went to chapel. Nobody expected to enjoy a sermon at church like they did at chapel. Most of it was above our heads, and yet, in a way, it was flattering to be expected to understand it all. At chapel they shouted a lot, and banged the Bible, and told stories that were quite funny sometimes, and used words that working people could understand, so that it was all a lot livelier. Mr Driffield never raised his voice, but went steadily on, and if he told stories they were out of a book and about the saints or something like that. It was all proper, and dignified, and meant to do you good, but dull. Nobody complained because that was the sort of thing you went to church for, though they did say that he ought to have known when to finish, which he never did. He would sound as if he was going to stop, and begin to move out of the pulpit, then he would say something more on the top step, and a little more further down, and so on, all across the chancel, and not finish until he got into his stall and gave out the hymn. If he went on too long Mr Du Cane would take out his watch and look at it carefully, before putting it back in his pocket; if there was much more of it he would unhook the watch from its chain and lay it down on the little ledge for the books in front of him. It was then that the Rector would start edging his way back towards his seat.

We didn't see much of the people at Byfield House except when they came to church, because Mr Du Cane didn't hunt or take an interest in anything, and his mother was too old. They didn't own any land, just the house and gardens, and a spinney or two, and some shooting. They were in London a good deal, or else abroad, and the servants used to say that Mr Du Cane hated Byfield and spent too much time with the whisky bottle when he was there, so that his mother was glad to get him away. But always, when they were at home, they came to church on a Sunday morning; and the service, and the congregation, and even the Rector became more important because they were there. The Rector always treated Mr Du Cane with respect, but he could stand up to him too, if need be. When he was going to turn old Jinny Tonge out of the lodge, because she was too rheumaticky to get out and open the gate fast enough for him, one day when he was in one of his tempers, Mr Driffield went to see him; and Perkins the butler, who was listening outside Mr Du Cane's study door, said he gave him a dressing down as if he was a little boy. All we knew for certain was that old Jinny stayed, and the groom had to get down and open the gate himself that winter.

The Rector, Mr Du Cane and, in a far off sort of way, Lord Postern were the gentry. They were the people who had the say. The world belonged to them. We knew them from the outside only, but still knew them well enough not to have more to do with them than we could help, or tell them too much about what was going on. The Rector was not quite in the same boat with the others; he was gentry, but he was a parson too, and it was a parson's duty to give help to those that needed it, and you could trust him a bit more than the others. People went to church, partly because the Rector expected them to and if you didn't go on a Sunday morning he would be round on Monday to find out why you were away, and partly because there was something about church that was more satisfying than there was about chapel. It was all orderly, and dignified, and decent. Nobody there talked about your sins more than was necessary, or wanted you to be converted, or prayed over you, as they were apt to do at chapel. Mother said church was the proper place to go to, but Father liked chapel better, he felt more at home there, so we had an interest in both places. It worked out very well too, because the chapel was quite a bit nearer, and easier to get to on dark nights. It stood just at the back of the Pheasant, up in the village between the two greens, with houses and light from cottage windows all the way.

On a dark November evening, when the grey drizzle which has afflicted the fields all day is turning to a nasty, penetrating rain, Mother decides that the road round to the church is too gloomy, and too dirty, and that it is a night for chapel. A family or two are outside the chapel door, waiting to go in, when we get there, but cannot make much progress at the moment because Selina Vear, from the shop, is having trouble with her umbrella. She is standing at the top of the steps, between the ornamental railings, wrestling with the thing and blocking all the doorway. It won't come down, and it won't go in, and Selina, backing her ample rear just inside the entrance so as to get out of the wet a little, is keeping everybody else out in the rain. 'Get it in edgeways, Selina, get it in edgeways,' says an impatient voice out of the murk, but the umbrella suddenly collapses, and Selina is inside, and the blockage is over. One of the chapel committee stands inside the little varnished entry place, and shakes hands with everybody as they go in, and a few people linger round the inner door for a few minutes' gossip. Within, there are rows of hard yellow seats running all across the room, facing a rostrum of pitch pine, highly varnished, furnished with three chairs and a large Bible. It is getting on for time to start the service, and the round, bald top of Mr Bilbee's head, with its fringe of black hair, is pointed at the congregation like the mouth of a cannon as he leans forward, shading his eyes with his hand, in a preliminary meditation. Mr Bilbee always does that, but strange preachers generally sit with their arms folded looking at what they have got to talk to, and giving the congregation a good chance to look at them. Two great oil lamps hanging from the roof, and a tortoise stove roaring its way through an armful of wood, make the place look cosy. We have a seat just behind the stove, where I can watch Barky Britnell stoking it up until the top glows red and the varnish blisters on the end of the seat beside it, and little beads of gum exude from the pitch pine, which can be picked off, and played with, during the service. Chapel is an easy-going place, you can do practically what you like there.

Mr Bilbee sits up, and looks round, like a man coming back to this world again. He stands up, opens his hymn book and, smoothing down the page, says, 'Brethren, let us sing to the praise and glory of God hymn number forty-one. "Salvation! O the joyful sound!"' He always begins with that, and Lily Painter starts working away with her feet at the old harmonium as if she is practising for a race. The harmonium has seen better days, and is not too well organized in its inside, so there is a good deal more knocking and banging in the music than you would expect, but that does not stop people singing. You sing at chapel, letting it come out as loud as you like, and not being over-hampered by the tune if you don't know it, but just keeping as near to it as you can get. Mr Bilbee makes a prayer, not like the church prayers, which flow on, rounded and beautiful, but just talk, rambling along about anything and everything.

The preachers at chapel changed a lot; you never quite knew who you were going to get. Now and then, the superintendent came over from Billington, but nobody made much fuss about him. Chapel ministers, it was well known, were just working men with a gift for preaching, which has been polished up at a college somewhere. They were not Oxford scholars like the Rector. But more often than not we got a lay preacher of some kind. There was Mr Chopwell, the printer, with bushy white eyebrows and a stiff white moustache, who shouted a lot, and banged the Bible. He would seem to be going on all right, telling people what sinners they were generally, then he would stop a minute, glare, and suddenly roar: 'It's all here,' thump. 'Here in the Word,' thump. 'Perhaps you never heard it when I read it, so I'll read it again,' a most tremendous thump, followed by some fiery passage or other. 'But some of you were asleep. You need waking and I'll wake you.' The whole Bible banged down on the rostrum with both hands, as if he was beating the dust out of it. And so he went on. The chapel committee asked for him not to be sent in the end. He was wearing out too many Bibles, with banging them all over the place, and some of the old people complained that you never knew when he was going to break out, and it was upsetting. But everybody liked Joby Smith, even though the stricter people did complain that he only had one sermon, one that was all about the loving kindness of the Lord. Joby kept a little shop in Billington, and went round selling tracts, and quarter pounds of tea. He was the only chapel preacher that Mother approved of. His goodness was of the quiet and gentle kind, and when he said, 'Praise the Lord,' during the service, which he did very frequently, he didn't shout it out like a defiance as so many of them did, but it came out gently, as if he really meant it, and it had broken from him unawares. Sometimes we got Mr Mabbet, the draper, and Mother never criticized him because he was a friend of hers, but she still thought Joby Smith the best.

If no preacher turned up from a distance then Mr Bilbee, who was the head of the chapel people, had to preach himself, and everybody thought that he made a very poor do of it. He liked to call himself a farmer, but he wasn't one really; all he had was three cows, and an acre or two of land, that he tried to get a living out of. The best times at chapel were when they had an anniversary or a revival meeting. There was always a lot of singing then, and people would give recitations, and it was more like a concert. Then they would have testimony meetings, when the chapel leaders got up, one after another, and described their state before they were converted; and people would sit there very interested indeed, hoping that something exciting would come out, but it never did. They generally stuck to a sort of formula about it, like saying that they had been the chief of sinners, or had been rollers in iniquity, or had wallowed in wickedness like pigs. Selina Vear, who was very fond of *Pilgrim's Progress* and liked to quote it whenever she got the chance, would vary things sometimes by saying that she had been in 'Beelzebub's orchard' a good deal lately; and those who were acquainted with the book would nod their heads, and look knowing, while all the rest would wonder what thrilling revelations about Selina's private life were being hid from them.

At its best, chapel brought independence, and a feeling that they had something of their own, into lives that were stinted of every other freedom. It comforted them with warm and beautiful words like Beulah Land, Jerusalem the Golden, and Redeeming Love. At its worst it was full of petty jealousy, and spite; with the hypocrisy showing through a worn veneer of religion, like the brass through the plating of an old spoon. Wherever you got it from, church or chapel, religion was a comfort, the only real comfort many people had. Crazy Barky

Britnell, sitting close to the chapel stove, and piling in the wood which he had spent half Saturday night chopping, lifted out of himself in an ecstasy of fire-making, or holding the hymn book he could not read at arm's length, and shouting unintelligible words to the tune, had the one happy hour of his week. Old Liza Bone, alone and half starved on parish pay, with her hands wrapped in the ends of her thin shawl; the battered old bonnet that perched on the back of her head pivoting on its strings and gently slapping up and down as she rocked to and fro while Joby Smith prayed, felt that there was a strong Goodness somewhere, who would look after her in the long run. That One Above, in some mysterious way, would see that life worked out according to His purposes and, in this world or the next, would make things come out all right. With religion life was never hopeless, or the loneliest without recourse. In the dumb misery which could not find words in which to express itself, or a listener with sympathy to spare, a stumbling sort of prayer loosened the tension round the heart. Dim and confused though the notion of religion might be, it held back despair. We might have been dumb animals, mere beasts of burden, so far as our ordinary life was concerned, but in church or chapel we knew that we were not.

Chapter 5

Barky Britnell had the one clay-walled cabin that was still lived in on the waste patch up by the top green. There had been a lot of this sort of house in the village at one time, but there were fewer people about now than there had been, and those that were left refused to occupy such places, unless they could find no other accommodation. Barky's was a squalid little one-storeyed hut, with the whitewash flaking off in patches from the outside walls, showing the yellow clay underneath festering like a sore. These cabins were all built in the same way, square, with just one room, a door and a bit of a window that held no more than two or three small panes of glass. There was no firegrate, but an open hearth that burnt sticks at the bottom of a wide chimney. What cooking there was had to be done in a three-legged, iron pot that swung from a chain hanging down the chimney. They stood up well enough, so long as the thatch was sound, but as soon as the wet got in the walls started to crumble, and the whole place fell to pieces.

Once or twice a year, when I came home from school, Mother would be bustling about, looking particularly determined and plainly working herself up to something. 'Don't you go running off to play. I shall want you in a minute. It's time Barky Britnell had a good clean up. I doubt if he's so much as put a broom in the place since I was up there last. What his poor mother would say if she could see him now I can't think.' So, with an armful of brooms and things, and a bucket for me to fetch water in, we set off. Barky's mother might well have been upset. He was a skinny little fragment of a man, in a couple of old jackets, made for a normal-sized man and swamping him, on the top of a grimy shirt; the jackets so rotten with age that they scarcely held together, a pair of cord trousers, frayed at the bottom and caked with filth. Two bright, brown eyes, wary and fear-filled, looked out from a mass of dirt and hair under a broken bowler hat. He didn't smell too good either. Some people wouldn't sit next to him in chapel because of that. Nobody ever called him by his first name, even if they knew it, he was always Barky. At the best of times his words came blurred and hesitant, but when he flew into one of his rages he just made hoarse, strangled sounds like a tormented animal. Some lout, who had worked him up and was enjoying the fun, showing off before other grinning louts one day, said, 'He is like a dog. Listen to him barking. Barky Britnell!' And so Barky he was.

Nobody, except Mother, ever got inside his cabin. It was his lair, his hide-away, his fortress. As long as he could keep it so, he had one place where he might be safe from his tormentors. It was firmly locked all day, and the dirty window, with its draggled scrap of lace curtain, made it impossible for anybody to peer inside. If the Rector called round of an evening, as he did on his usual routine, he never got in. Barky would stand in the doorway, with his arms spread across the entrance and the door pulled to behind him; never looking directly at the Rector, but watching him, furtively, out of the corners of his eyes. Never answering any of Mr Driffield's questions, except by saying, 'I be all right,' in a surly sort of way, and 'Thank 'ee sir,' a little more civilly, when finally the Rector's usual half-crown was put into his dirty hand. With his invariable courtesy, which would no more invade a poor man's house unwelcomed than a rich man's, Mr Driffield would not do more than wait to be asked in, and he never was. Barky paid his sixpence a week rent to Selina Vear at the shop, who owned the cabin, when he bought his few odds and ends there, but he never spoke to anybody else if he could help it, except when he was round at the chapel. There he was free, and safe, nobody would torment him. The boys who had started work but hadn't begun courting went about in a gang, and were generally referred to as 'them chaps'. Them chaps would get hold of Barky whenever they could, and badger him into one of his rages, and make him swear – gouts of filth in a torrent of screaming anger. Everything to do with Barky made me miserable; his loneliness, his pain, seemed to spill over on to me. All the cloudy sediment of fear that lay within me went swirling up and darkened everything when I thought of Barky.

He was coming up the road that spring evening, bent and plodding, his dinner basket on his back and his usual bundle of firewood perched on the top of it. He flung the wood down by the door and looked at Mother in an uneasy sort of way, not frightened, he never was of her, but like a boy who is going to have his face washed, but who still hopes it won't come to that. 'Come on now. Open this door. I haven't got all night.' Mother was always sharp when she was doing somebody a kindness. 'I've got to get the key, Mrs Hillyer' –

humbly. 'You should have it with you like sensible people do. Be quick and find it.' Watching us out of the corner of his eye, to be sure we were not following, or spying on him, he disappeared round the corner of his cabin, and came back with the key in his hand. I hated to go in. I had been there several times before, with Mother, and hated it more every time. Why did she insist on going? The place stank of fear and misery. There was a great heap of white ashes on the hearth. Without saying anything, Barky broke a few thin sticks over his knee, and started to poke about in it until he found a live ember. A small flame sprang up, and he nursed it with more sticks, watching with rapt attention until it grew into a blaze, but he was still uneasy about us being there. An old iron bedstead, pushed up into one corner, had a tattered blanket or two on it, and an old top coat. A chest of drawers, with all the knobs missing and the drawers half out, was on the other side of the room, and had on it a few grimy ornaments which had once belonged to his mother. An old wheel-and-spindle armchair, and a broken table, were all the rest of the furniture.

There was nothing in the way of covering on the hard-packed clay floor. But over the mantelpiece, where Barky could see it as he watched the fire, was a picture of a horseman in a red coat, leaping over a gate. The frame was filthy, and the edges of the picture speckled and brown, but the glass was wiped clean. He liked looking at that picture.

Mother was bustling about, over by the wretched apology for a bed. 'You'll have to do without these tonight,' and the filthy blankets went flying out of the door. 'It's time they had a wash. What your poor mother would say if she saw you in this state I don't know.' She seemed quite flabbergasted at the thought of it. 'She liked you, Mrs Hillyer, that's why I let you in. I wouldn't have any of them others.' His fire was burning strongly now and he was on his knees in front of it, caught up in it, living in it, oblivious even of Mother as she washed and swept and dusted in a commotion about him. But he got worried again the minute she went near the window. 'Don't you touch that, Mrs Hillyer. You'll only have them all peeking in at me, if you do that. I don't want people peeking in here. All they do is try to upset me.' His voice rose as the excitement grew on him, and his words started running together. 'Well, more shame them, and more shame you for letting them.' The dirty scrap of curtain came down with a quick pull, and a vigorous wet cloth went swiftly over the few small panes of glass in the window. She held the curtain at arm's length and looked at it with disgust. 'It's no use trying to wash this thing, it'll fall to pieces if I do.' Back went the grimy little bit of stuff, threaded by her capable fingers on to a new string, and stretched, properly this time, across the window. 'There, if you kept it like that, all that lot that have nothing better to do than look at you would have their work cut out to see anything. Don't you start swearing,' for Barky, carried away by the thought of his tormentors, was more and more losing control of himself. 'I am not going to have bad language. If your poor mother could hear you when you go on like that she'd drop down dead, poor woman, that she would.' 'I wouldn't if they didn't aggravate me,' he said, a little more quietly – he was always in dread that his bad language would get him turned out of chapel, and chapel was heaven to him. 'I'll kill some of 'em one of these nights,' flaring up again. 'You see if I don't,' and his rage tore at the poor bedevilled, grimy man, breaking out in wild talk and excited gestures. 'Don't you use such wicked words,' said Mother sharply. 'Killing people indeed! Put that poker down, and start getting your supper. There now, that's a nice little bit of pork you've got,' she went on, letting her voice sink to as soothing a tone as she could manage and dropping a little piece of fat belly-pork she had brought for him into his three-legged pot, where he had a few potatoes simmering already.

'He's getting worse and worse I do declare,' said Mother, rather flustered by his outbreak, as we went home. Usually, during these clean-ups, he sat quiet and bewildered, relieved but grateful when they were over. This time he sat staring at the fire and muttering to himself. I was glad to get away. The thought of Barky living his furtive life alone in the fields, or hidden in his dirty cabin, never speaking to anybody, rarely seen except at chapel, or plodding through the village, night and morning, to and from his work, was one to be rid of as soon as possible; but I couldn't help wondering what had made him like that, or if he had been born like it, so I said, 'Mother, how did Barky Britnell get to be mad?' 'It was a bad man as did it, my dear, and he'll be suffering for it now, you mark my words.' I didn't ask anything more. It was no use when she spoke in that tone. She would just tell me to be quiet, and mind my own business, if I did.

Father had come home from work and was sitting smoking his pipe by the fire, and it was getting dark. Mother bustled about to get him his food – she always had it ready for him when he came in, and it put her out that he had got home first. Father had been to Billington market with a cow that day, and hadn't had any dinner so he got a bit extra, fried potatoes and a little bit of bacon. Mother had her usual slice of bread and dripping and a cup of tea. She put the empty cup back into the saucer, smoothed down her apron and relaxed, ready to talk.

'I've been up to Barky Britnell's. He was carrying on something outrageous about them chaps. He's getting worse, I do believe.' Father wiped up the last of the bacon fat with the last of the bread, and said, 'Barky won't hurt nobody. They should let him alone.' Mother was worked up, obviously. She brooded for a moment, and then burst out, 'If old Arnison doesn't suffer for what he did to him there is no God in Heaven. I can't forget it! To see Barky as he was then, no more than twelve years old, a little pinched-up mite of a thing, going off to work in a morning with a face like death, it made your heart bleed. All that knocking about drove him crazy.' Father, placid with tea, said meditatively, 'Ah, Old Arnison was a tartar he were. A bad 'un, and no mistake! But Lucy should have stood up for the boy. Had it out with him.' 'Had it out with him!' Mother answered sharply. 'It's all very well for you to say that. What was she to do, left like she was? A child to bring up, and no sight or sound of the fellow to come by. How could she stand up to somebody like Arnison? If she got two or three shillings a week, going out washing, she was lucky. She wanted the money. The boy had to work.' 'So did I have to work,' said Father, 'everybody had to. I had a winter at Old Arnison's myself. But my dad wouldn't let me stay.

Cussing and swearing like a mad thing, knocking you about with his stick, and his fists too, if he felt like it. But he wasn't so owdacious down on me as he was on Barky. Many a time I've had his stick round my back,' he went on, quietly reminiscing, without any special sense of grievance. 'Whenever I see his old, red face and fat belly, jouncing about on that brown cob of his, I'd get out of his way, but you had to be slippy. He did it once too often to me though. My dad up and told him what he thought of him, and I went to work at Bratton's.' 'There was nobody to speak up for poor little Barky though, was there?' said Mother sadly. 'That's where a boy feels the need of a father. It should have been stopped.' 'I bet Old Arnison knowed as much about his father as most, and that is why he was so down on him,' said Father, with the air of a man who is pretty sure of his facts, but does not want to commit himself more than he can help. 'Barky shouldn't have taken it so hard. I had a sore back many a time, but it did me no harm.' 'But you weren't such a little bit of a frightened thing as Barky,' said Mother, impatient with that kind of statement. 'He used to be afraid to go home from chapel, if it was at all dark. He never had proper feeding. Lucy hadn't got it to give him.' 'Well, she shouldn't have let him stay there,' said Father, falling back on what seemed to him the common sense of the matter. 'He must have been forty year and more on that farm, it's all of twenty since Johnson had it, and he must have been with Arnison a good twenty before then. Kicked and cussed and knocked about for twenty year! It weren't much of a life.' 'And it ain't much now either,' said Mother. 'Five shillings a week is all he gets, and that ain't much to live on.' She knew how far, or how short, a way five shillings would go, if anybody did. 'Well, it ain't much, but who else would have him, even at that price? And he gets all his wood for nothing. Not but what he ain't a good worker, if you tell him what to do and leave him alone. He earns his money, and more, but who wants to have him about?' Father pushed his chair back from the table, and started to poke about in the fire with a twig to get his pipe alight again. Mother began to clear away the supper things, but Barky was still on her mind. 'He'll set that cabin of his alight one of these days,' she said, in a tone that suggested she was prepared for the worst. 'Such a man for fires I never did see.' The pipe was going steadily now. Father took it out of his mouth for a minute, and pondered the blackened bowl, while he considered whether he ought to risk his next remark. 'I expect, if the truth was knowed, he got his own back on Old Arnison after all. They never found out how that fire started, did they? And Old Arnison had got all his corn in that barn, threshed and ready to send to the mill. That cost him a pretty penny, I'll bet. He didn't last long after it, neither, did he? That broke him up, that did. He fretted hisself to death.' 'That's more nor you or anybody else knows,' said Mother sharply. 'They couldn't bring anything home to Barky, but he got the blame. He always gets the blame. It's time you boys went to bed. And don't you repeat what you've just heard your father say. You'll get yourselves into trouble if you do.' She pushed us off toward the stairs. Just as we were going up, we heard Father say, finally, 'No, they never proved anything. But you don't see Johnson letting him near the barn if he can help it, or the ricks either, unless there are plenty of people about.'

'John, did Barky really set fire to Old Arnison's barn?' I asked, when we were settled comfortably in bed. 'I don't know, but serve him right if he did. Barky likes fires.' I knew that well enough. Every Saturday night, in wintertime, you could find him in the little shed at the back of the chapel with a lantern, splitting wood, so that he could have heaps of it to pile on the stove next day, until the black turned to red with heat, and the little pot of water on the top boiled indignantly. Barky was lifted out of himself then.

Old Arnison's name was not forgotten in the village by any means. There was a great ugly, pyramid-shaped lump of granite over his grave in the churchyard, and people said that it was there to keep him down, because he was too wicked to rest easy. The writing on it did not support that opinion. In neatly cut letters, picked out with gold paint, it referred to him as, 'Walter Arnison, Forty Years Tenant of Lower House Farm. Greatly Respected by all Who Knew Him,' and went on to say that, 'This Monument was Erected by his Sorrowing Family'; and that, 'The Memory of the Just is Blessed.' One very wet winter the ground sank all round it, and some pieces fell out at the side so that you could see into the brick-walled grave, and there was the coffin, standing on end in a pit full of water. Old people said that it was a sign of God's judgement on him, but the Rector had the water pumped out and the tomb made good, so that everything was decent again.

Barky went on working at Lower House Farm when Johnson took it over. His pay was just enough to keep him off the parish, and for that Johnson got every ounce out of him that he could. Barky came to our house one winter evening in a terrible state. When we had got him quieted down a little, and could make sense out of him, it seemed that when he came home from work he had found his mother asleep on the floor, and he could not wake her. 'She is down there on the ground, Mrs Hillyer. I put her in her chair, where she always sits, but she keeps falling out. She won't wake up, Mrs Hillyer.' He was puzzled, and frightened, desperate for help. Mother went with him to see what it was all about. She was back in a few minutes for her best nightdress, and I was sent to fetch Liza Bone. Mother was rolling the nightdress up in some paper as I went out, and saying to Father, 'She can't be laid out in the rags she has got on, and there isn't a stitch of anything else in the place.' The parish paid for a deal coffin, and the Rector buried Lucy Britnell for nothing. Barky just stopped on in the cabin alone. Selina Vear didn't mind, so long as she got her sixpence a week rent. He went on working for Johnson just the same, and lived as he always had done. Only, as soon as the cabin was his, he never let anybody into it, nobody at all, except Mother.

Chapter 6

The summer after Grandmother was buried stands out above all the summers I remember. It is always there when I turn inward for it, and always with a radiance, a glow, that I can warm myself at though everything else has gone cold. All the separate incidents which distinguish it have a clear kind of delight about them, as if they were more perfect than such things have ever been since, and I saw them with some special understanding. It was a summer to rejoice in, taking it altogether it was the happiest summer I have ever known.

It was a famous summer for other people too, for it was the hottest that even old men like Johnny Batson could remember. From the middle of June till half way through September there was hardly any rain. The sun rose every morning in a grey-blue sky, and set at night unhampered by mist or cloud. The days were hushed and still, filled with the clear, hot sunlight. Even the cattle were too lazy to do much but stand in the shade and swish their tails, or lie under the trees chewing a thin cud. Haytime was over by the end of June, whereas some years it has hardly begun by then. It was a good crop, for it had been a wet spring, but once it was cut and carried there was nothing left in the fields. The lattermath refused to grow, for there was no life in the baked earth. The grazing died away from the fields which had not been mown, and only along by the ditch side, or by the brook, could the cattle find a full bite of grass. As the brook shrunk away from its banks, and they waded out through the sticky mud to look for weeds or tender shoots among the rushes, some of them got bogged down, and it was all that the men who found them could do to pull them out again. Farmers who had been pleased with themselves at getting the best hay they had saved for years, and who had talked about it among themselves as if they had planned it and could take credit for it, began to pull long faces and grumble that if this weather went on they would have to feed it all back to the stock, and be no better off in the end.

Poor people too felt the pinch, for the summer vegetables, which should have filled the cottage gardens and made a more plentiful diet, were thin and stringy. Peas hardly formed in the pod. Yet everybody was glad of the heat, and the sunlight. It dried out old, damp cottages and set ancient people out of doors in their armchairs, baking the rheumatism out of their bones. It was a change to get all the haymaking over so early. Where everything happens with an immemorial rhythm, it is pleasant to have that rhythm broken for once. The men who went with an old barrel on wheels to fetch water from the brook, for the stock in the fields where the ponds were dry, meeting others on the same errand, would say that they had 'never knowed such a summer', and that they ought to be hoeing or cutting thistles, and here they were at this job, carting water about; and there was a flavour of excitement in having something fresh to do, and something fresh to talk about. There was more standing about and gossiping everywhere that summer, and it made for friendliness, and a feeling that you were alive.

Week after week the glorious days went on. When school was over, the boys made for the stagnant pools left in the deep places along the brook to bathe, and splash about among the water lilies and the burnt up leaves that had fallen early from the trees overhead on to the dark surface of the water. There was the full, rich, sensual pleasure of lying naked on the short grass, until the skin was dry and prickly with heat, and then to plunge down into the quiet depths of the pool, among the long, smooth waterlily roots that caressed the body in passing like delicate fingers. That summer, Mrs Blore offered a prize of one shilling for the best bunch of wild flowers, brought to her each week by any child in the school. It was a bit of a mystery to us why she should want such things, but a shilling was a shilling, and we were all after it. It didn't do to take any kind of a bunch that you just happened to pick. She liked to have as many different sorts as she could get, so that it was quite a job to satisfy her. If there were any that she specially liked, she would draw them, and people said that they were printed in magazines. It was lucky for me that Father was about the fields a lot that summer, watering the stock, or looking to see if any cattle were stuck in the mud by the brook, where they were trying to get a drink; because he would tell me if he saw a particularly fine lot of wild flowers anywhere, or any that looked different, and I got the shilling a good many times. But she was very fair, and even if you didn't get the prize, she nearly always gave you a penny for bringing some.

Mrs Blore was a bright-eyed little woman, as brisk as a bird. She turned up, with two daughters, from nobody knew where, though some people said it was London, and bought The

Brick House, which she renamed The Beeches. It was pretty dilapidated when she got it, but after she had worked on it for two or three years, it was as nice a place as you could wish to see. Billy Makins did some bits of bricklaying on it, and painted the upstairs windows and the gutters, but Mrs Blore did all the rest herself. She had a way with the garden too, and laid it out afresh, and brought in some flowers that they hadn't even got up at Byfield House. It was a picture all that summer, scorching though the weather was, because she had a long rubber pipe from a pump in the backyard, and watered it every evening. Passers-by used to stop their gigs and dog-carts on the road, and stand up to look at it. Mrs Blore was a good sort of woman, for all her perky ways. She used to give a fair amount away in the wintertime to people who needed it, though everybody knew that she wasn't among the rich. But she was always one by herself, she didn't belong to the village. She went to church regularly, and Katie Blore, one of her daughters who was at school but was going to study music in London later on, used to play the organ sometimes, when she was at home; but neither of them went to the rectory much, and they only got the same sort of visits from the Driffields that everybody else got.

I was in and out of The Beeches quite a lot that summer, taking her flowers, and pumping for her in the evenings. I liked that, and used to hang about round her gate so that she would ask me in to do it. Not that I particularly wanted to work a pump handle up and down but, from where I had to stand, I could look into the house. I had never seen such a place before, it made you happy to look at it. The windows were all open to catch what breeze there was, and inside, in the drawing-room, there were books lying about, and easy chairs with bright coloured cushions, and pictures on the walls, and thin, summer curtains with patterns of flowers on them. It was a joy of a place to live in. The pictures were mainly of gardens, but there were some hazy sort of sketches of ruined buildings which set you imagining things about them. There was a big, flat piano in the room, which Katie played a good deal when she was at home, and I could hear the music as I stood pumping in the yard. It all fitted in, and made happiness; the hot summer, the garden, the curtains flapping a little now and then in what breeze there was, the lazy movement giving just as much life to all as was right. And there was Katie's music; it wasn't tunes, well, not the sort of tunes which Miss Lucy Driffield used to play at the Christmas concert, the notes just fell magical, resonant, spilled drops of sound that made a pattern in their falling; so that you had to listen to it working out, and something inside you seemed to fill with pleasure as you did so. They were lucky people who lived in houses like that. I wished I could.

The flower show that year was a thing to remember. It was always on August Bank Holiday, and as often as not it was wet. Then there was nothing to do except stand about in a dripping tent, watching people bring their exhibits in and trying to guess who would get prizes, or whose brown eggs would be disqualified because they had got their colour from being dipped in coffee, which was a good trick if it wasn't spotted. When the judges came into the tent everybody else was turned out, and there was nothing to do but go home and come back later on, to find out about the prizes. When that was over there wasn't anything else, and the whole year lost something, because there had not been a proper flower show. But in the hot summer everything was glorious.

Banking on the weather, the committee had arranged for a man to come over from Billington with a coconut shy, and there were stalls set out with things to buy. Besides the racing in the afternoon, the Rector had hired a band to play, and there was to be dancing on the rectory lawn until ten o'clock, which seemed very late to most. Ours was a wet garden as a rule, so we did well this year, when everybody else's was dried up. Dad was pretty sure of getting a prize with early potatoes, and nobody could ever touch our large, golden gooseberries. We had a bush of them that was famous. He let me take the potatoes and the gooseberries, and came along himself with a cabbage, and a couple of cauliflowers that he hadn't so much faith in. It is a tricky job taking exhibits to a show. People will stop you, and pretend to admire them. 'Them's fine rare gooseberries you got there, Dick. Your father'll get a prize with them I know,' pinching one to bruise it a little and putting it back out of its place to upset the arrangement, which was always important. Or, 'Your dad's got the best taters in the show, Dick,' giving one an admiring rub with a thick thumb, so as to loosen the skin a little, and make a brown patch come in an hour or so's time. But I knew about those dodges and kept my arm across the basket.

There was a bustle in the tent, as there always was, but another thing to make this year unique, Mr Wickens had taken his coat off! He was going about with an exercise book in his hand, ticking off the entries as he went from one exhibit to another, and he looked hot and flustered. He was the secretary of the show, as he was of everything else. His bowler hat was pushed to the back of his head, and he kept mopping his face with a large handkerchief. The sweat showed through his white shirt, in patches, all round his black braces. It was baking hot in the tent – if it hadn't been he would never have let us see those braces. Mrs Blore's other daughter, Cecilia, who was home from India where her husband was an officer in the army, had a kind of filmy lace frock on that was the talk of the village; and she said it was hotter than India, which made it certain that this was about the hottest summer we had ever had.

When the judges came, and everybody was turned out of the tent, they were pretty quick in getting into their best clothes and coming back again, because the band was here. They were sitting in a circle outside the tent, ready to begin. They had red coats with gold tassels on the shoulders, brass buttons, blue trousers with a red stripe down the sides, and blue caps with shiny peaks. It was the finest uniform anybody had ever seen. Their instruments flashed and glittered in the sun, the trombone especially, as it slid in and out, sparkled like a live thing. The band had even brought Barky Britnell out, and in his best clothes too, the ones he kept for the special occasions at chapel. The bowler hat he had on today was quite whole and, if the dust had been brushed off it, would have been a fairly decent black. His coat was an old shooting jacket that had belonged to Mr Du Cane's father, with round skirts and big pockets. Best clothes didn't run to different trousers, but with the idea of dressing up he had got a dirty muffler twisted round his bristly neck, hot though it was. He stood by himself, restless and suspicious, but like everybody else he couldn't keep away from the band. Nobody bothered about how long the judges took this year. Generally they stood about and grumbled that they could have done the judging themselves in half the time; but this year they were too occupied with listening to the music, and talking about the bandsmen, and wondering what the uniforms cost, to bother very much. There were people everywhere, and all of them enjoying themselves. It gave you a happy feeling to be with them.

The judges came out at last – Mr Hedges, the gardener from Byfield House, and a friend of his. Mr Hedges remarked to his friend, and to anybody else who might care to overhear, that it was 'A very fair lot indeed this year, considering, what with the weather and one thing and another, yes, a very fair lot.' The greenish twilight in the tent, the smell of the fruit and flowers and vegetables, the airless heat, made me feel as if I was in a tropical forest. There was a blue ticket for first prize on our potatoes and gooseberries, and a red one for second on our cabbage, so we had done better than we thought. Mother had first prize for plain sewing, she was safe for that, nobody could touch her at it. We had won about a pound! It was better than a week's wages. We were rich! 'This is a year, this is! Two fusts and a second!' said Father, beaming. 'You and John can have the second between you.' And he gave me eighteen pence right away. John won a shilling in one of the races, and although I didn't get anything like that, because I never was any good at sports, I had a special pleasure of my own too. It came from Mr Wickens. He was standing by the gate, smoking a cigarette and indulging in a word or two with Mr Bilbee, who was taking the entrance money. Mr Wickens had his coat on now and was looking himself again. 'Yes,' he remarked, 'the weather has been very extraordinary, very extraordinary indeed, Mr Bilbee. Everything is so dried up. The leaves already look quite autumnal.' Autumnal! I had never heard the word before. It had a good sound, a golden sound, a sound of colour, and ripeness, and the maturity of things. Autumnal! I said it over to myself a time or two, and wondered if there was anybody I dared try it on, and decided there was not. I should get hooted at if I did. I was in half a mind to risk it on Father, he liked coloured words too, but if they were to take his fancy they had to sum up a definite experience, something he could thrill over and talk about afterwards. Somebody told him once that the railway lines at Crewe were like a spider's web. He was fascinated with the thought. He knew what a spider's web was like, he had seen them, many and many a time stretched between brambles, or tall grasses, on an October morning, heavy with dew and shining as if they had been dipped in glass. The thought of railway lines being like that quite entranced him. Whenever anybody mentioned railways, he would tell them about it. 'The railway lines at Crewe are like a spider's web.' But I never thought it was necessary to stick to any one particular picture for words. You just had to let them have their way with you. They were spells to call up glowing visions. They goaded the imagination. They could bring together shreds and remembered pieces of scattered pleasures, and make them into one delightful whole. Autumnal was everything rich and splendid, and aflame with colour, in the dying summer.

The rectory lawn was large and level, with smooth turf surrounded by many-coloured flowerbeds and thick shrubs at the back of them. Dotted about among the flowers and the bushes were dozens of little red and yellow lights; small, bright and quivering with life, as if the dark was backed with flame which was struggling through in pin points. Miss Lucy had spent hours putting little glass jars, with night lights in them, in places where they would show and yet look as if they had got there casually and by accident. The band sat under a big old cedar, in the middle of the lawn, and each player had a jam-jar, with a bit of candle in it, hanging by his music book. The players were in the dark, so that it looked as if the music was coming of itself. The drawing-room windows, with lamps standing in them, and the stars, far away and faint in the summer sky, gave light enough for the dancers. Older people stood about and gossiped among themselves for an hour or two; and then went quietly home in threes and fours, keeping one another company, and finishing their talk on the way. The Rector was enjoying himself. Bare-headed, with his red velvet smoking jacket on, sometimes he puffed at his cigar, and sometimes held it in his fingers while he talked to somebody, until it was nearly out, and he had to get it going again; he went about joking with people, asking after their families and hoping they had been having a good time. At ten the music stopped. There was a shuffling about and pushing back of chairs, while the players shut up their books, stood up and straightened themselves. Then they crashed into 'God Save the King', playing as if they meant it, with plenty of thump on the drum. There were three cheers for the Rector, and the lawn emptied, couples going off arm-in-arm into the quiet night; the rectory lights went out, and there was just the shadow of the great cedar tree lying, a vague fanciful shape, across the lawn, and the smell of trampled grass. I saw the last bandsmen climb into the wagonette, shut the rectory gate behind them, and went home soaked with satisfaction.

Chapter 7

Two or three times every summer we went to see Uncle Daniel; it was always on a Sunday evening but we never quite knew when it would be, because Mother never would make up her mind until the last minute. He was her Uncle Daniel really, and the visit was supposed to be hers, so naturally she settled when it was to be. There was no woman about his place, he was a bachelor or a widower, I never knew which. But everything was clean and tidy, and the patched smock frock which he wore (he must have been the last in our part of the world to do so) was always well washed. His house was about a mile and a half away, in a little hamlet called Keloe, which was too small to have a school or a church, and just had to make do with a Methodist chapel, a shop and a beer house called the Green Man.

A Sunday or two after the flower show, just as we were getting ready for church, Mother said decisively, 'We will go and see my Uncle Daniel. The parson can talk to himself tonight.' She knew that strictly speaking that would not be so, that some other, less significant people than ourselves would be there, but that was the proper formula for announcing a visit to Uncle Daniel. One of the things to be careful about was that nobody else in the village knew anything about this until it was over. Not that it mattered particularly, but it was all a part of the elaborate operation known as not letting other people know your business. What the business was didn't matter very much, it was not letting other people know it that counted. When you succeeded you were one up in a contest that went on continually, if you brought it off at all regularly, that proved you to be quite a superior sort of person. People talking about you, and wishing to say something particularly praiseworthy, would add, 'And they are not the sort that lets everybody know their business, either.' Father, as he said many times, was a man who 'believed in going to a place of worship on a Sunday', but he always agreed with a visit to Uncle Daniel. On a hot summer evening he'd as lief spend the time in a walk through the fields, and a talk with Daniel at the end, as sit in church.

The first thing to do was to get through the churchyard without anybody stopping us and saying, in that aggravating way which showed that they had caught us out, 'I expect you'll be going to see your Uncle Daniel, won't you?' If Mother had not made up her mind until late, when the congregation was going in, it was rather a job, but it could be managed. The thing to do was to wander quietly through the churchyard, over to the far corner where the path to Keloe started, stopping to look at the headstones on the way and so giving the impression that you were just passing a few minutes looking at the graves, which was an approved occupation on a Sunday evening. Then you slipped quickly through the kissing-gate and were out of sight behind the churchyard hedge. After that, the strict decorum of Sunday was relaxed, and John and I were allowed to wander about a little. There was always a chance of finding an abandoned lark's nest in a tuft of rank grass, or a pewit's nest, empty and deserted in the late summer, but not useless finds, for John would remember to an inch where they were, and the old birds might come back to somewhere about the same spot next year.

At the end of the first field the path led over the brook across a little rickety, white wooden bridge, and here also it was permitted to lag behind and hang over the rails for a minute in the hope of catching sight of the wary old jack who lived in the dark pool beneath, and defied all attempts to catch him; thinking at the same time how delightful it was to be doing this instead of sitting on a hard, shiny oak seat in church, with Mother giving you a poke if you so much as move, or happen to catch the wooden kneelers with your heavy shoes, and make a clatter. Our countryside had no hills, only rolling billows of land that rose and fell in wide slopes. Keloe lay at the top of one of these. There was never anybody about. Those who were not at Byfield church, or with the Methodists, sat at home until the service was over. Past the Wesleyan chapel, set back a yard or two from the road behind two laburnum trees; and you could hear the preacher's voice through the open door, without being able to make out the words. Past Fincher's shop, where the blue blind was let down to indicate the Sabbath rest, but caught up, as often as not, at one corner on a jar of pickles or a tin of salmon, and showing a few desperate flies diving underneath it and climbing up the glass in a futile effort to get out. Then along a narrow path with a privet hedge on one side of it, and a pond on the other, through a little home-made gate, and there was Uncle Daniel's house.

It was a low, single-storeyed place, with whitewashed walls and a heavy thatched roof. It was not easy to see it at first, because of the apple trees that grew on one side of the path, and the peas and runner beans that grew on the other. There was a flowerbed, about a yard wide, underneath the windows, and a little walk that went all round the house. Uncle Daniel owned the place himself and spent all his time keeping everything trimmed and clipped and weeded, so that it was as neat a garden as you could wish to see. This hot summer evening he had brought his armchair out into the garden, and sat there smoking his pipe; a heavy old man, with a red cotton handkerchief over his bald head to keep away the flies. He never moved when we reached him, but just said, in his slow, old man's voice, 'I thought you might be coming up. Fetch a couple of chairs out here, Bob. When you get a summer like this you don't want to waste it sitting inside. You boys go and look round the garden, but don't interfere with anything. You can get yourselves a few pea pods, if you like, but don't touch anything else.'

It was cool and fragrant among the pea rows, but there were not many pods fit to get. Uncle Daniel knew that well enough when he sent us there. We soon gave up looking for the ones there were. John started to dig out a mole run that he found, but I didn't think he stood much chance of catching the mole at home. It was pleasant just to stand there, with the green and the fragrance all around. I heard Father say, from somewhere on the other side of the pea rows, 'So Jack Boldin is dead is he? Did he leave you that picture of his?' 'Ah, his wound got the better of him in the end. The picture is up in the house.' Then

I knew that I must see that picture, whatever happened, because it was famous. A lot of people knew about it, but very few had seen it. Slipping in by the back way was easy enough, and there it was. It was hanging on the wall, opposite to you as you went in, so big that it took up all the middle. A real oil painting, in a gold frame, something worth going to see. It was called *The Soldier's Watch*, and showed a dark plain, with hummocks scattered about it, and in the distance a line of hills. In the middle of the picture, so that it seemed as if you were standing in it, was a little round fortification of stones and earth. The stones were painted very clearly, and the earth looked as if the lumps of it were so dry that they were crumbling away. There were the dying embers of a fire, and grouped round it were half a dozen grey shapes that were supposed to be men asleep under their blankets. A figure in uniform, with a moustache and a battered topi, stood with one foot on a stone, nursing a rifle and gazing out at the dark landscape under a sky that was thick with stars. You could see that he was tired and had been fighting all day by the look on his face, and the way he stood; besides, his uniform was all torn.

I knew about that picture. It was painted by a friend of Uncle Daniel's, who had gone for a soldier and fought in the Zulu wars, and it represented an experience of his. He had been wounded and come back home, where he had limped round the villages as a postman for some years, until his wound got too bad and he had to give it up. Then he started teaching himself to paint, helping out the shilling or two a week that he got from the government by occasionally selling somebody a picture of their house, or of a bunch of flowers, or a local view of some kind. This was his great work. He had done it slowly, and carefully, with the best of his skill, in the last months of his life, when he could no longer go outside his house. Perhaps he had waited till then so that the picture should be the best that he could do, and his feeling for it be heightened by the thought that he, and this recollection that lay at the centre of his memory, would soon disappear together. So he had given all that remained of his life to it, experiencing once again, with all the vividness of a dying man, some lonely night on the veldt; when the silence, and the danger, and his sleeping comrades, and the awe of the African night, had fixed themselves as permanent things in his soul, and become that part of him which he most wished to remain when all the rest of him was dead. A confusion of thought and feeling bubbled up in me as I looked at it, mixed with something like pain. He had thought about this all his life, tasting, again and again, the fear, and the weariness, and the chill of it, never getting rid of it, never perhaps wanting to do so, but treasuring it as the supreme moment of his existence, turning it over and over, and looking to see if it had any meaning. And there it was, on the canvas in front of me, standing up out of the past like a man wounded but living, rising up from among a heap of corpses. The man I used to see limping along the lanes with his letter bag had carried all this about with him, just an ordinary man, but with something inside him that made him different, and separate. Perhaps he talked about it sometimes, as old soldiers talk about their fighting, but never really telling it, leaving that for his last days, and then laying it on, stroke after stroke, in this new-found art of his, so that something of what it had meant for him was there for me to see.

Through the open window I heard Uncle Daniel say, 'We must have a walk round the garden. The apples won't come to much this year; what with the flies, and the dry weather, they won't be worth picking.' Chair legs scraped on the path. They were going through the proper ritual of a visit. For a minute or two they would wander round; Mother admiring everything, and Uncle Daniel pretending that nothing was much good, then they would come inside. It wouldn't do to stop. There would be a row if I was caught in the house, when I had been told to go into the garden. I slipped out, and let them find me when they went to look at the apple trees.

Uncle Daniel said, 'Sit down again for a minute. I think I've got a drink o' beer somewhere in the house. I'll go and see.' He had a barrel of it, as we all knew well enough, but he always said it like this, if he was going to offer them any. If he was in a bad mood he wouldn't say anything about the beer, and then, as we walked back across the fields, the visit would seem to have fallen rather flat. He disappeared into the house, and came out carrying a white jug with a blue band round it, which held four glasses full; one each for the three of them, and the other to be shared between the two men. I never knew why he was so much better off than the rest of the family, but he didn't work for anybody, and he didn't take parish pay. It gave us status in Byfield to have such a relative.

That summer was a particularly good one for the blackcurrants, and that was lucky for us, too, because we had twenty or thirty bushes of them, set round the edges of the garden, and they brought in money. Sometimes we could make enough out of them to buy Father a good strong pair of boots for the winter, or something Mother might want. Picking them was a pleasant thing to do, sitting there in my shirt sleeves, with an old sun hat on, feeling, somehow, free, and the drowsy afternoon sounds all around. Mother started first, and stripped the currants from the upper branches, and I followed her along and picked those at the bottom of the bush, and in the middle, because, being smaller, I could get at them better. Twice a week the currant buyer came with a two-horse yellow van, which he stopped on the top green, and he turned his horses loose to pick a bit, with their traces hitched up over their backs, while he dealt with the people who had currants to sell. He was a plump man of about thirty, with his hair parted in the middle and plastered down. When he arrived he had a collar and tie on, and a smart jacket, but this year he took them off, rolled up his shirt sleeves and opened his waistcoat, before dealing with the heavy skeps of purple fruit, which he stacked, tier on tier, in his van. Most people felt that this was a pity, for he was a dressy man, and his get-up much admired; but they had to admit that it was sweaty work this year, lugging all those currants about.

There was plenty of the fruit too this year, so there were lots of people on the green, joking with the currant man, and thinking of the money they were going to get, and gossiping. It was something to remember, and talk about, as the man weighed the fruit, poured the currants out of the baskets and buckets people had brought them in, out into the round wicker skeps, and stacked these in piles on his van, so that in the end his two horses would have quite as much as they could deal with on the way back. The buyer was always laughing and joking, too, 'joshing the old women along', as he said, while he weighed what they had brought, glanced quickly at his scales, which had the dial turned towards him and away from the sellers, and explained that there was less than they thought there was, and that prices were down this year because of the glut, and that he would get into trouble with the factory for paying as much as a penny a pound when other vans were bringing them in cheaper, but he didn't mind getting into a bit of a row, if he left satisfied people behind him who would sell him their currants again next year. Nobody knew what the factory did with the currants. There was talk that they were made into a blue dye, but most people thought that was a waste of good fruit, and wouldn't be allowed.

The hot days came and went, unchanging in their bright regularity. Water was getting very scarce, and the parish council locked the pump, except for two hours in the evening, because some people were fetching water from it for their stock, and everybody was afraid that the well would run dry, though Johnny Batson, the sexton, who was the oldest man in the place, said he could never remember that happening. As a sort of parish officer he was given charge of the padlock and chain. At five minutes to six, he would come stumping up the road with that peculiar walk of his, that put all the weight of his body on his heels, his worn-out, old, flat felt hat, shapeless and bleached with years of being wet and dry, his corduroy trousers patched at the knees. Tucking his stick under his left arm, and teetering on those painful feet of his, he would search in his pockets for the key, enjoying this moment of importance and disregarding the chaff of the waiting men. 'It's all a lot of foolishness, a lot of foolishness. This here well ain't never run dry in my time, and it ain't going to run dry now. There now,' as the chain dropped to the ground, and with a sudden reminiscence of a phrase heard in chapel, and suitable for the occasion, 'Let the water of life flow free!' That was a fine, dramatic way of doing things, and he must have been glad that he discovered it. Every night I waited for Johnny to come out with his 'water of life', and he always did. Locking the pump was quite a pleasant thing too, in its way, because everybody had to fetch their water about the same time of an evening, and so they could stand about and have a bit of a chat. There was more of that sort of thing this summer, in one way and another, than there had ever been before. But of course some people grumbled at the parish council for interfering.

It was an easy harvest too. Wheat cutting was always done by piece work, so much an acre, and the men who did it generally reckoned on losing a few days on account of rain or drizzle, and that meant less money for the job as a whole. But this year there was no break, and the dry weather for weeks before meant fewer weeds and the sheaves were lighter to handle. It was hot work, out in the middle of the field, with a blazing sun beating down on your bent back all day. Still, it made it seem all the better when the time came to sit down, on the shady side of a shock of corn, at midday, with a jar of beer or a can of tea; and eat a hot dinner out of a basin, while the women who had brought it stayed and had theirs with the men, because it was so nice to be out of doors in such weather. Father was a good man with a fagging hook, and was never slowed up in the afternoon with the weight of too much beer at dinner time, as some of the others were. All day long he went steadily on, the swing of his hook as fast and rhythmical in the evening as it was when he started in the morning. It was a pleasure watching him, as I stood with a handful of straws for a band, waiting to lay it at the right moment for him to drop the sheaf into, then to tie it, pressing down on the bundle with my knee to make it tight. At any moment the swinging hook might cut open the little ball of dried grass that was a field mouse's nest, or send a young rabbit scuttling further into the standing wheat; until they were all concentrated in the last half acre, and the boys stood by to knock them on the head, when they were driven out at last, and there was the certainty of young rabbit for dinner.

Cutting beans was a hard job that year. The hot weather had left the pods so dry that the shock of the hook, as it struck them, rattled half the beans out on the ground, so that they were wasted. They had to be cut very early in the morning, while the dew was on them. It was a queer feeling, being woken up in the middle of the night, and walking a mile or so through the shrouded fields. Half of me was heavy with sleep, and the other half gripped by the chill strangeness of that time. Bean bands were hard to make. You had to lap the ends of two separate handfuls together, and give them a special twist; if you didn't get it right the band fell apart. When mine broke, because I was too drowsy to bother with it, or because the knack failed me, Father would drop his hook and twist one in a second, saying, 'Dowie', his special oath, and the only one he ever used, 'I never see such a boy. I might as well do it myself.' But he was never angry, and I think he really wanted me with him for the company, more than anything else. At that time in the morning, out in a wide field, anybody would feel that they wanted company. The silence, and the strangeness, made you glad to be with somebody. Everything seemed alive, yet only half visible, and very still. The first sheaf or two came slowly, as Father shook off the sleep which the heavy work of the day before was pressing upon him, but soon his hook was crashing among the thick stalks with its usual steady swing. The hours went by unnoticed, yet all the while the feeling of having invaded a secret world, of kind, and yet unearthly life, was as pervasive as the night air. The scurrying of small animals, alarmed in their nocturnal pursuits, the raw, rough smell of the cut bean stalks, the changing light as the moon went down, and the starlight and the dawn met together in a luminous haze, filled a charmed time that lapped the edge of the world's mysteries.

Then it was broad day, no one stirring. Soon the cattle began to move, grazing their way up towards the gate where, when the sun was well up, the cowman came to call them in for milking, the first human sound to break into this man-deserted world, and wake it to normal life. Father threw down his reaping hook. 'It ain't a bad night's work,' he said, as he looked back with an approving eye over the row of bean sheaves that lay, in a straight line, behind him on the stubble. Then, as if he had noticed it for the first time, 'It's a rare morning,' and he added, as if he was sharing some special thought with me, 'It's always purty at this time of the day.' Slinging his coat over his arm, he picked up his rush dinner basket and we went home. He was asleep as soon as he sat down in his armchair. Mother sent me to bed till school time, but what was the use? The night and the morning possessed me.

Chapter 8

Mother had not been too well lately. Whether it was the heat, or what it was, her energy flagged. She got tired, which was unusual for her, and sat down for a minute or two sometimes, even in the middle of the morning, which was unheard of. Never a great eater, her appetite failed altogether. It looked as if she was going to be ill. Father, who, for all his slow way of talking, was quick at noticing things, began to get worried, and fussy; but Mother said there was nothing the matter, it was the heat, she would be all right when the weather got cooler, and it couldn't go on much longer like this. She would be all right.

But she wasn't. The weather broke suddenly, at the end of September, with heavy thunderstorms that rolled and crashed across the village and disappeared over the horizon in great inky, black clouds. As the weather cooled, and the thunder stopped, it settled down to rain, day after day, the steady drops beating the dried-up leaves from the trees before their time, so that they blocked the gutters and the ditches and flood water spread out on all sides. Everybody was moody and depressed. Mother got no better, and it worried us, because she was the pivot on which all our lives turned. What would happen to us if she was to fail? I do not know if it would be right to say that I loved her, in the way children usually love their parents. She was always, in a sense, strange to me. There was something withdrawn about her. She never trusted you with her whole personality, as Father did. My feeling for her was something sharper, and deeper, than that. I know how much I suffered when she suffered. When she was at her wits' end, and going without her own sparse requirements in order to scrape together some necessary shillings, it brought pain that cut my heart to pieces. And yet her hardness frightened me, and all the more because, in some dim way, I sensed that it was her only protection against hurts that she could feel, though Father could not. It never bothered him in the least that we were looked on as poor and ignorant, and seemed at everybody's mercy. He was what he was, and that was the end of it. He had no wish to assert himself against his circumstances. The great fear of Mother's life – getting into debt – never troubled him at all. If he had to owe a little money, well, he had to, he could trust to his own honesty to pay it, some time or other, and people could think what they liked. But for her it was torture to owe a penny. It seemed to put her in the power of those she owed it to, and it had been her passionate endeavour, all her life, to be free of other people's impertinence and scorn. Within her narrow circumstances, no one should look down on her. For anyone to have found her house dirty, or her children's clothes unmended, to put herself within reach of any slight, was torture. Yet it was torture she could not avoid, for the poor must always suffer slights.

Whenever I try to recall her to memory, it is the picture of her at this time that comes most easily to mind. It is afternoon. The monotonous rain is falling outside, and I am indoors, because there is nothing else to do, and nowhere else to go in this weather. The dinner things have been washed up, the house swept, and the fireplace tidied. Mother has washed herself, done her hair, and put on her afternoon blouse. She had got down last Saturday's *Lloyd's Weekly News* from where it rests all the week, neatly folded into four, behind the lamp on the chest of drawers. Her little hard wooden chair has been placed a bit nearer the fire. She unfolds the paper and begins to read, at the place where she left off the afternoon before. In a minute or two she starts to nod, and then, as if she chooses rather to surrender to the drowsiness than be overcome by it, she folds the paper again and lays it on the table by her side, and then, leaning her head on her hand, sinks quietly into a little sleep. As the muscles relax, her face loses its firmness and looks tired, and hopeless. For a moment or two she stays like that, her resolution withdrawn, her heart defenceless. Then, a little at a time, the face tightens again, her eyes open, and she sits for a minute or two with her hands folded in her lap, looking dreamily at the fire. Then, with a quick movement, she gets up and begins to bustle about, hard and resolute again.

For some days it looked as if Father was making up his mind to say something important. He was not a man for getting ideas – as a rule, he left that to Mother – but this time he seemed to have produced one. With the subtlety of the simple he waited for the right time to bring it out. It was Sunday evening. We were just back from church. I was reading *The Pickwick Papers*, in a battered old copy a boy at school had lent me. Mother and Father sat, one on either side of the fire, in their best clothes. She was in a mood to listen. He gave three or four quick puffs at his pipe, as he always did when he was getting ready to say something important, then, boldly, as if he knew that there would be opposition but he would be proved right in the end, he said. 'Why don't you go up to London, and see your brother George?' It was out, the great idea. 'London! What's the man talking about? We've got no money for London,' she answered sharply, and yet it was easy to see that the idea appealed to her too. 'We've got money enough. It's the best year we have ever had. There is the show money, and the currant money, and harvest was all right too, and I've got a bit to come for the beans. We shall be five or six pounds to the good. You can afford it all right.' He said 'you', because spending money was her department, as his was to earn it. 'And what shall we do about the rent, and some new clothes? If we don't put a shilling or two by when we can, we shall never have anything. You never know what you may want,' and, her permanent worry, 'If you had a long illness, what should we do then?' 'We've always done all right, and we shall again,' Father answered stolidly, refusing to be side-tracked, but getting at the same thing from a new angle he added, 'Your brother George would be glad to see you, I'll be bound. Take our Richard with you. John and me can manage all right.' That was really crafty, he was getting her at her two weakest points, London and her brother George. 'It would be eight and six for the fares, him and me together,' she answered, and you could see she was going to give in. This was interesting. I was going to London! Mother had told us a lot about it when we were small. She had lived there before she was married.

When her father died she was only eleven, the eldest of five children. Granny had to find what work she could to keep them; if she had gone for help to the parish they would have sent her to that prison for poverty, the workhouse, and she would have let them starve rather than put that stigma on her children. So she went out washing and cleaning and, if there was weeding or harvesting to be done, to work in the fields. But housework paid best, she got ninepence a day for that, and her dinner; sixpence was all that could be got for a day's work in the fields. Mother was left at home to bring up the rest. She never liked to talk about that time, or think about it, if it could be avoided. She scrubbed, and washed, and cooked what food there was for them all, and began as a child to carry the same sort of responsibilities she would struggle with all her days. During that time there settled in her child mind – where it came from was a mystery – the fierce determination that she, and hers, were to be looked down upon by none. Though they were poorer than the poor they lived among, they would keep their hardships to themselves, and suffer neither pity nor scorn. They would tell no one, though their stomachs were empty and the cold pinched them. They would beg from no one, they would whine to no one. So she washed, and mended, and racked her brains to make the few pennies that came into the house meet the barest needs for keeping alive.

At thirteen she went to London, as servant of all work to a grocer's family at Clapham. Nathan Gregory, the carrier, used to go up to London once a week with butter, and eggs, and poultry, and he got her the job with one of the shopkeepers he supplied. So she set off from home, comforting herself, in her frightened loneliness, with the thought that she would see

Nathan once a week, and not be cut off altogether from the people in Byfield; but she never did, because he only called at the shop, and she lived at the house in Clapham. All her belongings were in a battered old brown tin hatbox. But the grocer's wife was good to her. She had plenty of food, and was worked no harder than she would have been at home. She even began to save a little money. At eighteen she married Father. They had been children together, and ever since they could remember had known that they would get married some day. When he was ready for her she went, and started again the old life of making ends meet, and holding up her head in a world that was resolute to beat it down. She still hoarded a few treasures from the Clapham days, a necklace of flat, oblong jet beads, which was the only piece of finery she had ever spent her money on, and a silver brooch, shaped like a horse shoe, with a huntsman's whip and horn fastened across it, which Father had given her as a love token. They were kept locked up in the tin hatbox, with two or three pairs of old lace gloves, which she had accumulated somehow, but never worn, her best hat and the burial policies. London remained resplendent in her memory. It was a promised land, a place of plenty. She had been young, and secure, and happy, working twelve hours a day in the grocer's family. Her stories to us, as children, were about the splendour of the shops, and London Bridge, and the river, and fashionable people going to church on a Sunday morning.

Out came the hatbox again for our London journey. With that, and a large bag of assorted vegetables, because it was well known, in our parts, that London vegetables were not worth eating, we climbed on to Bill Gregory's old blue van; the very same van that Mother had ridden away in as a child, so many years before, but shorn now of the glory of two horses, and trundled along by one gaunt old brown cob who was too old, too tired and too bored to take much notice of Bill's cluckings and slappings of the reins on his back. The carrier's business, like the van, was not what it had been. There were no more weekly trips to London, only a Wednesday and Saturday jaunt, with a few parcels and a passenger or two, between three or four villages and Billington market.

Bill was all set to find out where we were going; Mother, as good as ever at the game of not letting him know until she was ready. We settled down on the seat beside Bill, its hardness softened for our benefit by two or three folded corn sacks. 'You'll be getting down at the Two Brewers as usual, Mrs Hillyer, I expect?' he remarked, opening the battle the minute he had clucked and slapped the old horse into motion. 'Well, no, I don't think we will Mr Gregory, not today. We'll go a little bit further with you, if you don't mind,' said Mother, pleased at having got him going so early. 'Whereabouts then? Up in the market square?' 'Well no, it would suit us better if you were to put us down a bit nearer the station.' 'Sending that lot off to London?' looking at the sack of vegetables, but rather puzzled by the hatbox. 'Yes and no, as you might say,' said Mother, a little sharply. It was too early to be pressed as closely as this. Bill let it rest for a minute or two, while the bony horse put his head down between his front legs and slowly hauled the van up the rise, out of the village. 'Going off yourself for a bit then?' asked Bill, coming back to it when we got to the top and were jogging along again at the usual pace. 'Just for a day or two,' answered Mother, knowing the end was in sight, but keeping it up as long as she could. 'That train at four o'clock, stops all the way up to London, so they tell me.' 'It'll do us all right then, if it does.' Bill was now in a position for the final shot. 'Your brother George will be glad to see you.' 'I dare say he will. It's ten years next month since he was down here last.' It was out, and both of them could relax. The tone now was easier, more normally conversational. 'Your brother George done a good job for hisself, going up to London like that. I'd a gone with him, if I hadn't had that fool notion of going for a soldier.' 'George had it in him. He'd a got on anywhere, our George would,' returned Mother with quiet pride. She never blamed Father for staying where he was, or for his unambitious ways, but George represented enterprise, push, success. Going up to London once, with some horses which his master had sold to a brewery, he had got himself a job in the same firm as a drayman, and now had risen to be foreman, in charge of all the deliveries, with a house over the stables and as much free beer as he liked. Occasionally he had to visit markets and fairs, buying horses for the firm's drays: he was a successful man in every way.

Paddington station, for all its size and bustle, looked a dismal place. The rain had come on again while we were in the train, and now dripped through cracks in the glass roof and stood about in dirty puddles in the roadways. 'I don't expect your Aunt Caroline will have the sense to come and meet us,' said Mother as we struggled along the platform with the hatbox and the vegetables. But she was wrong. There was Aunt

Caroline, standing by the wicket, a dumpy woman in grey. At home Mother always referred to her as 'Poor Carline', and spoke of her with the kind of pitying contempt which she might have used of a feckless child. All the troubles in Uncle's ménage she put down to the inability of 'Poor Carline' to rise to the heights demanded by such a man as her brother. Why he had ever married such a poor, pitiful thing as her she could never make out. But today, in the first flush of seeing her again, and in return for her coming all the way to Paddington station to meet us, she was granted the stiff politeness Mother allowed to important people.

We jogged along in a cab through the wet streets. If this was London I didn't think much of it. The murky weather made it dark early, and the shops began to light up as we went along. We were winding about through back streets, where everything was small and grubby. Here and there a butcher or a fishmonger stood leaning disconsolately in his doorway, looking at the weather and wondering, no doubt, if there would be any more trade that night. People scuttled along the pavement, their heads down in their coat collars, bumping into one another, getting their umbrellas mixed up and hurrying on again; or dashing across the road underneath the horse's feet, which slithered on the slimy wood blocks, as the cab man reined him in to avoid knocking somebody over or running into some vehicle. If this was London it did not come up to expectations at all. It was too dark, too dirty, too full of scurrying people looking as if they were running away from something. We got out of the dismal little shopping streets into an area of warehouses, high, dark places, deserted in the early evening. The cab turned in through a brick archway, with a gas lamp hanging from it, and there we were in a yard, with drays and empty barrels all about.

A man was standing at the top of some wooden steps, which led from a door in the second storey down to the stables, cursing somebody in the yard below in a loud, fluent and bullying fashion. I guessed it was Uncle George, though it was too dark to see clearly, and his language was a bit of a shock, for Mother hated swearing. He was heavy and tall, over six foot, and in the gloom, with the shadows cast by the gas lamp, he looked huge. He stopped his flow for a minute to call out, 'Come on up, Liz. Leave them things. The yard man will bring them up,' and then went on bullying the person below, but the edge had gone off it, or so it seemed to me. Mother obviously decided to ignore the swearing. She gave Uncle George a little peck on the cheek and pulled me with her into the house, out of the way. There was a naked gas jet flaring in the passage, and the place smelt of gas, and horse, and stale food. 'He does go on so at the men,' said Aunt Caroline weakly, as she started to take off her things in the untidy living-room; trying to placate Mother, who was not at all pleased at what she was running into. Mother made no reply. Nothing would have induced her to criticize her brother to Caroline, not with a house like this; and she ought to have kept him in better order, anyway.

Uncle George came in after a minute or two with a yellow glazed jug in his hand; a marvellous yellow-glazed jug, with a brown elephant on it, and the name of the brewery round the top, partly hidden by overflowing froth. He greeted her kindly, and in a rough way seemed fond of her, and glad that she had come. He hadn't forgotten the time when Grandmother had been out all day, scratching a living, and this sister had been father and mother and everything else to him. I went to bed that night in a dark little room with a sooty window high up in the wall. Through the cracks in the floorboards the stamp of horses and the rattle of halters running through the iron rings of the stalls came up clearly, and with it the all-pervading smell of horse.

There were two lines of stables, one ran along the ground floor, underneath the foreman's house, the other was in a basement, completely below the pavement. They looked best in the early evening, when the long lines of magnificent animals were bedded down for the night, and the scent of fresh straw, for a time, dominated all other smells. The flaring gas jets lit up the round, sleek rumps. Men who had been out with the drays all day were putting on their coats, and talking among themselves, as they got ready to go home; the night men, who would polish the harness and get everything ready for the next day, were just coming on duty. The proudest moment of all was at eight o'clock in the morning, when the great horses, their coats glossy, their manes and tails braided, their bushy fetlocks all combed out, their harness shining, and the drays washed clean, were lined up for Uncle George's inspection before they were sent to the loading bays. The drivers were looked over as carefully as the rest, for the brewery prided itself on a smart turn-out, and a man who came without a shave, or with torn clothes, would be cursed down from the high seat, where he towered above the beer barrels, and be lucky if he only lost a day's pay and not his job. The brewery paid good wages and had the pick of the carters, who were expected to be a credit to the firm. Not until everything was passed as satisfactory were the huge vehicles allowed to roll away and pick up their loads.

As soon as the last one had disappeared, the yard settled down to quiet. One or two horses that were being rested were led out and given a handful of hay in a corner while their stable was cleaned. Uncle George went off to his little cupboard of an office without a window, where the gas flared all day, and spent his time among samples of corn, bottles of horse medicine and dirty lists that were scattered about everywhere. If dealers looked in, as they did sometimes, the yellow jug came and went a good deal, and then Uncle George wouldn't have much to say at mealtimes, and be a bit unsteady on his legs, and Mother would look down her nose at him, and be sharp with Aunt Caroline. There wasn't much for me to do but hang about, or go out with Aunt when she did the day's shopping. In a sort of way, I think she liked me. It must have been a change for her to be with somebody who wasn't pecking at her all the time. She took me for a ride on a motor bus, and let me see Hyde Park and Buckingham Palace, and showed me things in shop windows that she liked. I quite enjoyed being with her. Mother sat indoors sewing most of the time, because Aunt Caroline never mended anything, but we went over to Clapham and saw the house where she used to live, though there wasn't anybody there she knew. I was glad when the week was over. Evening was the worst time, when the drays came home. Uncle George stood by the archway as they came in, running a quick eye over them to see if any damage had been done, or anything gone wrong during the day. He could spot at once if a driver had been misusing his team, beating them or pushing them along too fast to make up for wasted time, and then there was a row. If the man was of a surly nature, or had been drinking too much, he would answer back, and they would swear at one another, and perhaps come to blows, though not many of them wanted to risk a fight with a man of Uncle George's size. But this cursing and threatening made everything feel miserable.

The glamour fell away from London for me during that week. I think it did for Mother too, though she never said anything about it. Her brother bought her a thick winter coat for a present when we came away. He got it off a fat man with a hoarse voice, a friend of his, who kept a stall in a market somewhere, and came in one night with three or four over his arm, so that she could take her pick. It pleased her very much. 'Our George is good-hearted, he always was,' she said, when she showed the coat to Father, as if that made up for some unspoken criticism which lay at the back of her mind. A day or two later a barrel of the brewery's best beer arrived, and we were much envied by the neighbours. That was my first glimpse of what went on outside Byfield, and I was not impressed.

Chapter 9

My last winter at school was quite pleasant, in spite of not knowing what was to happen to me when it was over. There wasn't much point in going over, again, the simple stuff the others were plodding through, I was well ahead of them, so Mr Wickens left me to myself in general, just giving me books to read, English history and literature mainly, and teaching me a little geometry when he had the time. Once or twice he said something, in a half-hearted way, about me sitting for a scholarship at Billington Grammar School, but he did nothing about it, just left it to me to take up the idea or let it drop as I liked. I let it drop. Not that I didn't want to go, I did very much, but it wasn't as simple as that. I could think of nothing better than to go on learning, and Billington Grammar School was a famous old place that any boy would want to go to if he could. It stood in a quiet street, up near the church, a three-storey building, hundreds of years old and graceful to look at, its warm red brick emphasised by white window-frames and a noble white door, with a long polished brass bell pull alongside. Anybody would be glad to belong to such a place, but it was five miles away and to get there I should have to have a bicycle, like the farmers' sons who rode there every morning, and I should need special clothes too. Mother would have got them somehow, I have no doubt, but knowing how she had to scrape to get every penny above the bare cost of keeping alive,

I couldn't let her do it. So I said nothing at home about Mr Wickens's idea. If I had mentioned it I shouldn't have had a choice, I should have had to go.

I didn't fancy the idea, either, of riding to Billington everyday with the three boys who did go. They were all farmers' sons, who had been to our school. They were not very bright, but their fathers paid for them to go to the Grammar School, because it was where better-class children went, and they might make friends with some who were well-off. Those three would take it out of me, in some way, if I got a scholarship. Just bullying wouldn't matter, I could stand up for myself against them any time, but to tag along, ignored or talked at, would be misery. They had enough money to spend, and could buy their dinner at school every day; and whatever other miracles Mother could work, I couldn't see how she could manage that one. I would have to take my dinner with me, and be laughed at for having a dinner basket, like a labourer. Laughter is a deadly thing for a boy to face. I couldn't, so I said nothing about the Grammar School idea, and Mr Wickens, I think, was not sorry. The schoolmaster in him made him suggest it, but the cautious man in him, the man who wanted a quiet life, was glad that it was not taken up. If it had been, the farmers, who had to pay for their sons, would have had something to say to him about giving working people's children ideas above their station; and wasting the country's money on people who had no right to what they couldn't pay for. Still, the idea twisted and turned and rankled about in my mind all the early part of that winter and made me miserable, not knowing what to do. In the end it died of itself. Mr Wickens said no more and I kept quiet.

The changes of the seasons, the budding, the blossoming, the falling of the leaf, and the winter's chilled, slow pulse were in the nature of us, whose forefathers had tilled the soil for so many generations. They conditioned us, as they conditioned the earth we lived upon. Winter crept into the veins, numbing and darkening the senses. It brought a chill of mind and body, which poor food and patched clothes were unable to overcome. The small, ill-built cottages were whirlpools of icy draughts; the one door, opening directly into the one living-room, let in the raw outside air every time it was opened. Our house was better than some, because we had two doors and a little sort of entry between them; but the old, rotten window-frames, ill-fitting doors and decaying brickwork were still but poor barriers against the cold. The only time when it was near to comfortable was after tea when the fire, which had been made up with a chunk of wood and some wet slack, began to burn clear and throw out a steady heat. When she had finished tidying up, Mother carefully adjusted the wick of the tall glass oil lamp, which was her particular pride, so that it gave the best light it could without smoking, put her chair beside it, got out her sewing and settled down for the evening. Father stretched out his legs to the heat and smoked his pipe, dropping, in a ruminative sort of way and at infrequent intervals, the pieces of small news he had picked up during the day. There was comfort in the air. John always had something of his own to do in a corner, making a bird trap or a whip or anything else that let him use his hands.

It was my best time for reading, but books were running

short. I had borrowed everything there was to borrow round about, and there was nothing left but a waste of Sunday School prizes, unread and unreadable. But just when the situation was looking desperate, Mrs Blore started to help. From pumping for her in the summer, I had slipped into doing odd jobs about the house and garden. One day, when she had been clearing up and had some rubbish to burn, she gave me an old copy of *Waverley* that was pretty badly torn and falling out of its cover, so that I could get the fire going. I had read a chapter or two of it already, in one of the little books that Mr Wickens used to give out on a Friday afternoon, and I was passionate for the rest. You don't use gold mines to light fires with. I laid this one down, where I thought she wouldn't spot it, and got the blaze started without it, but she spotted it all right. 'Here's the book. Why didn't you use it as I told you?' she said sharply, picking it up and flicking the pages through her fingers, as if she was half a mind that it was worth saving after all. 'I thought I'd like to read it, ma'am,' I answered, as meekly as I could, because it would be heartbreaking if I lost it after all. 'Read it? Why, whatever do you want to read a book like this for?' 'I read some of it at school, ma'am, and I wanted to finish it.' She finally made up her mind that it wasn't worth taking back and threw it down on the ground, saying, 'Well, you can have it, if you want to.' So I took it home, and the evening was aflame with delight. Mother, who was good at that sort of thing, patched it up so that it was quite tidy again. It was the first real book of my own that I ever had, and I have it still.

That I was reading Scott must have caught Mrs Blore's

fancy, because she lent me the rest of the Waverley novels, one after another, that winter. She was a good sort, really, though a bit sharp. She never wasted a thing, but she would give away money or anything else provided she had made up her mind about it, and intended to do it. The time after tea was something to look forward to all that winter. Sitting in a kitchen chair, with the book flat on the table in front of me – that way you could get the best light – another world came in, a many-coloured, sounding world of knights and travellers, and paragons among women, and rascals who were all that rascals should be, came in and pushed everything else aside while they played out their play. It was hard to leave them when the time came to face the icy bedroom upstairs. It was agony getting into a cold bed, with chilblains that had been comforted in the warmth below but started all over again between the chilly sheets. But the furious itching would pass off in time, and then the luxury of lying warm, between sleeping and waking, and imagining the outside world, strange in the night and cold. Imagination, which has been stirred and stimulated all the evening, thrusts me out into that world. I am a robin which has been lucky enough to find a crust of bread by somebody's door, and now dozes in a sheltered corner, snug, fed and satisfied. I am a sheep, heavy with wool, drowsy in the centre of the flock on the frozen turnip field, the stars clear and cold, the breath of all the sleeping animals lying above them in a thin vapour. I am the old jack, hanging silent beneath the ice in the pool by the bridge, impervious to the cold, solitary among the roots of the bullrushes and the water lilies. I am all these, their lives and mine one, until sleep blots us out.

As the days grew dark and winter settled down, heavy and dead, the human spirit itself seemed to shrivel, as the vigour of all growing things shrank back into the earth. Deadness and monotony took hold, broken only by an occasional concert and by Christmas time. For the men, the tempo of work was slower. Those who were about the cowsheds and the stables found the animal warmth of those places a comfortable thing; but those who had the grim job of looking after the sheep penned out on the frozen turnip fields, dragging heavy loads of hurdles across fouled and trampled ground, as the pens were moved each day on to a fresh patch of roots, hated the winter and wanted it over as soon as they could. For people like Barky Britnell, hedge-cutting all the winter, wrestling with great bushes, heavy with rain or snow, standing in wet ditches with patched and leaky boots, it was a harsh time. Once or twice every winter there was a concert. The Rector got them up, and read pieces from Dickens or Pett Ridge. Katie Blore played the piano if she was at home, not enjoying it apparently, but in a curious, abstracted sort of way, as if she was thinking of something else at the time. But even the people who complained that she never played any tunes, not proper tunes, tunes that people knew, had to admit that she could make the old school piano pretty well talk. Billy Makins was always the star turn. A builder by trade, he was a comedian by instinct; and though some of the chapel people said that his tales were not fit to hear, the Rector said that there was no harm in them, and laughed like anybody else. It was surprising how a concert cheered you up, people would talk about one for days afterwards.

But the big days, the days that everybody looked forward to for weeks, were St Thomas's Day and the Christmas tea. St Thomas's Day was special, it had been Byfield's big day for a couple of hundred years. Its celebrations were started by Dr Randall, who had been rector once, a long time ago. There was a monument to him in the church, with a long epitaph in Latin underneath a woman in a flowing robe, who was leaning on an urn. When he died, all that long time ago, he left a farm to the parish, so that the rent could be spent for ever on clothes and bread for the poor on St Thomas's Day, which is the twenty-first of December. It was all in charge of two trustees, appointed by the Rector, and he always chose himself for one and, in a very fair-minded way, Mr Bilbee from the chapel people for the other. They settled that the money was to be used for children's clothes, according to the value of some tickets, which had to be got from the trustees, and they were very strict about not giving these out to anybody but parents. If children went for them, they were sent home without any, and told to tell their parents to come themselves and show a proper respect to the trustees. On St Thomas's Day, in the evening, the two of them sat in the school to examine the things that had been bought, so as to make sure that the money had been spent properly, and to give out the bread. If any parents tried to get anything for themselves off one of the tickets, they were in for trouble.

It was exciting, going up Brandy Hole Lane, with the light from cottage windows making the dark places between seem darker. The school was all lit up. People were going in with bundles and parcels, and all their children with them; partly to help carry the bread home, but also to be counted, in case the trustees forgot how many there were in a family. You could smell the bread as soon as you got into the school lobby, crisp, new and appetising. It wasn't often that we got whiff of that delicious smell, because what the baker brought round was stale, people liked it that way, it went further. But this was hot out of the oven, good, big cottage loaves; each with a smaller lump of bread sitting on top of a larger one, twice the size of ordinary loaves, though some said that was because the baker put too much water in at these times, as he contracted by weight. Mixed with the smell of bread was the smell of new corduroys, of new shirting, and the heavy, greasy smell of cheap cloth and cheap shoe leather; all of it fighting its way through a general smell of school, which is made up of chalk dust and grubby books and bad ventilation.

The trustees sit behind a trestle table, the Rector looking very dignified, his well-brushed black clothes and white hair showing up nicely in the lamplight; Mr Bilbee, a bit uneasy and a bit defiant at being in such company, rather edgy, as if he might quarrel with somebody at any minute, but relieving his feelings by twiddling a copper seal, which he wears on the end of his watch chain. Mr Wickens, secretary as usual, sits a little to one side, ticking off the families, as they come forward, in a big book. It isn't done for the women to go up to the table in a bunch, they go one by one, taking their children with them; the rest, who are waiting their turn, stay at the back of the room. Nobody is in any hurry, and it would be poking your nose in if you show any curiosity about what other people have bought before they are willing to show you, which they are certain to do in the end.

Some woman comes up, slaps down a brown paper parcel on the bare board of the trestle table; opens it, a little apprehensively, holding the string in her mouth so as not to lose it, while she uses both hands to spread out the clothes she has bought, and then stands back to wait for the verdict. Generally the Rector says something pleasant, about what a good bargain it is, or what nice stuff it seems to be; then the woman wraps up the parcel again, looking relieved and rather pleased. If the clothes happen to be for a girl, and whoever bought them has gone in more for finery than solid wear, he will just nod and say nothing and everybody knows that he doesn't approve, and they won't rest until they have seen what it is; and then they will say to the mother, who is generally a bit defiant about it, 'You did right, a gal ain't like a boy, she needs a bit of something to make her look nice,' but when she has gone home they will say, 'Ain't that like her! Wasting her money on such rubbish.' Mr Bilbee just sits there and twiddles his watch chain, and apart from speaking to his chapel people when they come up doesn't say much, but tries to look dignified like the Rector.

Every year it happens. We know it will, and wait for it, nobody is going home and miss a show like that. People hang about after they have shown their clothes and got their bread, pretending that they are just having another word or two with somebody; but though they do not say anything, everybody knows what they are waiting for. Willie Potter comes in, holding a little girl by the hand. Willie used to be a footman at Byfield House at one time but now he keeps the Pheasant, though he doesn't get much custom and has to help out by waiting at the farmer's ordinary, at Billington, on market days. He knows what everybody is waiting for, and it sharpens him up a little. If they want a show, they shall have one. Everybody stops talking and watches; they are quite excited, but you couldn't tell that by looking at them. Willie marches down the room, pulling the little girl along with him, slips in front of a woman who is tying up her parcel, and stands before the table. Mr Bilbee looks uneasy, the Rector just the same as usual, quiet, unruffled. The little girl is Willie's granddaughter, she is about seven or eight and called Gwendoline, which is a very fancy name for our parts. Her mother is said to be married and living in London, but although she comes home sometimes, dressed up to the nines, her husband never does, and Gwen's name is Potter on the school register.

Willie just stands there, in front of the table and the trustees, holding her by the hand, and waiting to be spoken to; the waiter in him struggling with the rebel so to speak. 'Well, Mr Potter?' the Rector says, knowing perfectly well what is coming. 'I want to know what my little Gwendoline has done, that she hasn't had the charity again this year,' says Willie, standing very stiff and speaking with dignity. 'You know as well as I do, Mr Potter, that the rules say the charity is for the children of the labouring poor, and you are a public-house keeper, you are not a labouring man. She is not eligible.' 'I'm a working person, and I work for my living, like everybody else,' replies Willie, letting his temper begin to get the better of him. 'I know you don't like me, neither church nor chapel, I'm nobody, I'm not, just because I keep a public house, but I didn't think you would take it out on my little Gwendoline. You've got a down on that child, that's what it is. And what harm has she done you? Just a little child like that. I shall see a solicitor about it. She is going to have her rights.' Willie sounded quite fierce. 'I wish you would, Mr Potter,' says the Rector as calm as ever, 'then perhaps we should not have a repetition of these extraordinary scenes every year.' 'My little Gwendoline has as much right to it as anybody else,' says Willie, tailing off a little, knowing that he was not going to get any change out of the Rector, and knowing, too, that there wasn't much he could do about it. He always talked about his 'little Gwendoline' as if she was something fragile and fairy-like, but she was a great lump of a girl, with a dirty nose and a torn pinafore generally. 'I'm afraid I can't help you, Mr Potter,' says the Rector, having had about enough of it. 'You must stand aside, we have other people to attend to.' Mr Bilbee never said anything on these occasions, but once or twice he had remarked afterwards that the parson was too soft by half, and that one of these days he'd tell that damned greedy Potter where he got off; but everybody knew that he never would, because for one thing he would have lost his temper, and when he did that he used bad language. He always said at testimony meetings that swearing was his thorn in the flesh, and if he had let himself go in public, in front of the Rector and everybody, the chapel people would have had something to say about it, and his wife would have been upset, so he kept quiet. The Rector nods to the next woman in the line, who pushes forward with her parcel. Willie Potter goes off, white and determined-looking, dragging his little

Gwendoline and stalking contemptuously past the loaves of bread as he goes out, as if he wouldn't have touched one, even if the trustees had gone down on their knees and begged him to, though there is no restriction on the bread, and he can have it if he likes.

The rest of us went home, with the loaves piled up in our arms, crisp, sweet and appetising; with the lovely feeling that there was new bread for supper, and that the clothes had been passed and were now our own without question, and that it was a fine thing to belong to a village like Byfield, which had such privileges. Nobody thought that they were accepting charity from anybody, it was all part of our rights. Dr Randall was a Byfield institution, and we were Byfield people, so it all belonged to us. The Christmas tree was different, that was charity, in a way; and a few of the stricter chapel people wouldn't have anything to do with it, but nobody else cared, it was a change, and the gentry got enough out of us, so why shouldn't we get something out of them once and away?

Lord Postern gave the tree itself, and Mr Bond, his agent, used to talk as if it was a forest. Mrs Du Cane used to give five pounds, to buy the presents that were put on it and to pay for the children's tea. The Rector paid for a meat tea for their parents out of his own pocket, and Miss Lucy did all the work. Once or twice a week, from about the middle of November up to Christmas time, she used to go off to Billington in the pony and trap, and go round all the cheap shops, buying things. She was a good soul and never minded how much trouble she took. When you went into the school on the night there was the tree, all lit up, with coloured candles, and strings of twinkly, shining stuff stretched all across it, weaving in and out among the presents, and a great silver star at the top that shone like the star of Bethlehem. It was the prettiest sight of the year. When we were all sat down, Mrs Du Cane herself would come in and go all round the tables in a dreamy, far-away sort of fashion, saying nice things to the children and the people who were helping, in a gentle, old kind of voice, and smelling of perfume. Mr Du Cane went with her, helping her through the tight places between the tables, not saying anything himself, but looking pleased, as if she was saying the things for him. When they had been all round, Mr Wickens would take out his folded white handkerchief, smooth his moustache to either side with it and, pulling himself upright, say, 'Boys and girls, give three cheers for Mrs Du Cane, the very generous provider of these lovely gifts.' When that was over, Mrs Du Cane and her son drifted off, and we were free to talk and enjoy ourselves. The presents were distributed after tea, stockings and scarves, and gloves, and things like that, and that was the end of the first part. All the children under twelve were sent home to bed, and their parents told their big sisters to watch them and see that they didn't get up to any tricks, because they were going up to the school to the meat tea.

That was the Rector's affair. Anybody who cared to come could have beef, and ham, and bread and butter, and cake, and things like that, as much as they could sit down and eat. Even Barky Britnell turned up, with a little of the dirt washed off his face, and sat down at a corner of one of the tables, and said nothing to anybody, but enjoyed his tea all the same. There was a concert afterwards, and while their parents were eating and the room was being got ready for the entertainment, the girls helped with the washing-up, and the boys were turned into the school yard out of the way. It was a clear night, with the beginnings of a hard frost. Some of the boys were boosting one another up to look through the misted-up windows and find out what was going on inside. There wasn't much in that, I knew what was going on, people were just having their tea, that was all. Turning away from them, I saw the village and the fields; the houses shrinking back into the shadows, strangely clear in places, blurred and indistinct in others, the fields lying white in the frost, dead and empty. By daylight I knew every inch of them, but this was different, strange and haunted seeming. Anything might come out of it. And something was coming. I heard it, faint in the distance, and listening as it came nearer, I thought that it sounded like a horse and trap, but not coming along smartly, as it should have done, and it seemed as if there were two horses. It stopped opposite the school gate and a man called out, 'Hi, you boys!' He was a stout man, standing up in a gig, with a big overcoat on with the collar turned up, and a bowler hat. 'Hi, you boys! Come over here.' I could see now that he had another horse tied to the back of the gig, and it wasn't liking it. At any minute it might wrench the rail off with its furious jerks. 'What are they up to in there?' said the man in a thick voice, he sounded half drunk. 'Stuffing theirselves with the parson's grub?' Nobody answered. It was a statement of the obvious, and needed no answer. 'One of you boys go in and see if anybody wants to earn half-a-crown, leading this blasted colt to Littleboro.' Nobody answered, until my brother John, who was standing just in front of me, said, 'Who shall I say it's for?' 'Tell them it's Joe Pounder. They'll come. They all know me.' That was true enough, everybody knew Joe Pounder, well enough not to want to do him any favours. Littleboro was six miles away. Who would want to go there, at this time of night, and with a wild colt like that? John and I went into the school lobby and signalled to Father. 'What colt is it?' he asked when we told him what was wanted. 'It's that white-faced one of Johnson's, the wild one.' 'Well, tell him he can take it himself,' said Father. 'I ain't walking no twelve miles tonight, for no half-crown, and then not get it as like as not. No, tell him I've got my best clothes on, and don't care about going.' He corrected himself, not wanting to send a rough message to a man like Joe Pounder, and get us into trouble. Nobody else would go either. Joe Pounder was not popular. He had a little bit of a horse-dealing business and talked big, but he had been in court cases more than once. 'None of 'em will come,' said John. 'Then this devil will have to come as he is, if he pulls the gig apart,' said the man in an angry voice. The colt blew violently, nostrils distended, and the breath coming in a white cloud. It was wild-eyed and frightened. 'I'll take him,' said John, in a matter-of-fact sort of way. 'Well now, that's a boy!' said Pounder, relieved that he had got his problem off his hands after all. 'Untie him. I'll go on ahead. You know the way I expect.' 'I can find it.' 'Half-a-crown for you, my boy, when you get him there,' Pounder went on, as if he was promising a fortune. He settled himself down on the seat, wrapped the rug round his legs, and with a cut at the horse in the shafts, dashed off into the night.

John soothed the frightened animal for a moment, and then gently led him away after the retreating gig. The muffled clop, clop of the colt's unshod hooves on the hard ground sounded ominous. It was staggering! It did not seem possible that John should do so foolhardy a thing, and yet there was his small figure, alongside the uneasy colt, disappearing down the road in the moonlight. 'Your John will get himself killed, that's what he'll do,' one of the boys said gloomily. 'That colt pretty nearly broke old Johnson's leg last week, that's why he sold it.' Fear was surging up in me. The cold outside was nothing to the cold that was churning about in my inside. What should I do? If I could get Father by himself, I might tell him, but he was with Mother, and if she found out there would be an explosion. I couldn't get them out of the concert without a fuss, and children were not allowed to sit with their parents, they were always put right in the front row, under Mr Wickens's eye, to stop any larking about. So, miserably, I took my seat, hoping for a miracle. Perhaps the colt wouldn't hurt John after all. The concert went on. I heard bits of it, not much; the greater part of me was in a sort of fog, out on the Littleboro road, a cold, clammy fog full of fear. The Rector read a piece out of *Oliver Twist.* Billy Makins had everybody roaring. I could even hear Mother give the sharp little cry that was the nearest she ever got to a laugh. People coming out told one another that it was the best concert they ever remembered. It had taken about two hours, and a wild hope started to grow towards the end, that if John had a bit of luck and got a ride home, he might be back before it was over. But that couldn't happen. There wouldn't be any luck, that hateful beast had trampled on him already. He would have been waiting outside if he had got back, and he wasn't. 'Where is our John?' said Mother as soon as she had got away from the rest of the people. 'He's gone to Littleboro,' I answered miserably. 'With that horse? Good Lord Above, he never has! Bob, did you hear that? Our John is taking that horse to Littleboro,' she said, hard and angry. 'He shouldn't have done it. He should have come and told me first. How long has he been gone?' Father answered, and even he sounded anxious. 'He went while you were having tea, and I couldn't come and tell you because I couldn't get near you.' I knew that was a lie, I could have got to them if I had tried. I wished now that I had, no matter how much fuss it had caused. 'I'll go and see what he is up to,' said Father, turning back toward the road. 'What's the good of that?' Mother replied sharply. 'If he's been gone two hours he will be there by now, if he ever gets there,' and I knew that, angry as she was, she would not have John shamed by sending his father after him when he had undertaken to do something by himself.

Their fear fed the fear which had been gnawing at me ever since John went. If they were worried, there was something to be worried about. They didn't bother to send me to bed. Mother made some tea in silence, and we sat waiting. The slow minutes ticked by, with a hollow sound, in the tin clock on the mantelpiece. 'Our John's good with horses. He takes after your brother George,' said Father, breaking the silence on what he thought was a hopeful note. 'He had need be,' answered Mother grimly. All the shining joy of the day collapsed, it was misery from start to finish when such a thing as this could happen on it. And it was all my fault. I was the one who had caused it. I should have begged John not to go. I should have told somebody, and got him stopped. That road to Littleboro was the darkest and loneliest anywhere about; there were not more than two or three houses in all its length; nowhere to go to, nowhere to get help. For the first time in my life fear, real fear, laid hold of me, to shake and tear my heart. It was quite certain that the colt would kill my brother. It was happening. I could see it – the colt's sudden rear, the milling forefeet crashing down upon John – the beast's mad rush away into the night, and the still figure lying smashed and dying in the middle of the road; the dark trees moving, ghost-like, in the wind overhead, and not a soul to find him, until the red life had all drained out on to the frozen ground. My mind raced in the creation of horrors and there was nothing I could do, nothing anybody could do. If it would only come back to six o'clock again, so that I could stop it all happening!

Father got up and went outside. He left both doors open, and I could see him halfway down the garden path, standing listening. After a while he came back and sat down again, uneasy, but saying nothing. 'If anything happens to our John,' Mother burst out, 'I'll tear that Joe Pounder to bits with my bare hands.' To see her iron self-control go like that was terrifying. My heart prayed in broken misery, 'O God, make him come back safe.' 'I'll go out along the road a bit and see if I can see him,' said Father, unable to sit still any longer, and this time Mother did not try to stop him. It was worse with him gone, and just the two of us sitting there, listening. Everything seemed to mean that John was dead. It was five hours since he went: unless something had happened it could never have taken him all that time. It was all my fault. I should have gone with him. I wouldn't have been any use with the horse, but I could have got help, done something. The doors were still open, as Father had left them: neither of us wanted to shut out the earliest sign of any news that might come. But there was only stillness. Then the church clock struck eleven, clear, silvery, deliberate in the frosty night; thrusting home, like an icy spear, the length of time since the rattle of Pounder's gig and the clop, clop of the colt had disappeared into the moonlight.

The garden gate clicked. Somebody was coming up the path. Whistling! There was John, his face red with cold. He held out something in his hand towards Mother. 'I got that half-crown,' he said, and there it lay in his palm for her to take. 'Where is Dad? What have you got the doors open for?' Then Mother did to John what I never knew her do to any of the rest of us at any time, she flung her arms round him, and kissed him, and the half-crown rolled away beneath the table. Father came back in a little while, and heard the story. He had missed John up by the green, where the road forked. It had taken a long time to get to Littleboro because the colt had to be gentled along a lot at first, but it had quieted down and hadn't been any real trouble. Mrs Pounder had given John his supper before she let him start back, and that had taken time, and he had walked all the way and was tired. It was a wonderful day again.

Chapter 10

John was small, dark, quick and bright-eyed. He was quite fearless in everything to do with animals, and they had no fear of him. He was not interested in books. All his inclinations, and his gifts, were for outdoor pursuits, and companionships with beasts and birds. The thoughts and habits of living things were clear to him, without any effort at all. He had not to reason what they would do at any time or in any situation, because he was sympathetic to their instincts, and knew in his bones what they would do. To me he was a wonder. How could he possibly understand such things? We were brothers, but there was more than brotherhood between us, a special relationship, that was entirely satisfactory to us both. We were two people, as different as could be in our ways and thoughts, and yet each perfectly accepting the other. He would listen to my confidences without understanding them or trying to; just taking them as coming from me, and no doubt making sense so far as I was concerned, but outside his sphere. Not treating them as trivial, because they were not his own; listening to them patiently but making little comment, and taking them just as a part of me. He was the outlet for all the odd notions that milled about inside me, and all the better outlet because he made no effort at all to influence me.

I was big for my age, slow, clumsy and timid in all the things that he was so good at. If I went with him on one of his expeditions, which I did now and then, he was pretty sure to send me home before long for making a mess of something which he had given me to do, and explained patiently how to do, and although I might be angry about it at the time, the anger never lasted. It made no difference, he had his ways and I had mine, neither could be the other, but we were sure of each other, that was what mattered.

We had an elder brother, who was working as an under-gardener at a great house near London – the Rector had got him his job – and there was Ellen away in service. But neither John nor I wanted to be gardeners, and it wasn't easy to see what else there was to do. I had no ambitions at all, John had two, both of them impossible it seemed. If he had been able to have his way he would have chosen, above everything else, to be a gamekeeper. To spend all his days about the fields, and in the woods and spinneys, would have been pure bliss. He would have treasured every pheasant and every partridge; known the run of every hare and every rabbit. But there was no game preserving at Byfield House in these days, though there had been in old Mr Du Cane's time, with great shoots, and parties that went on for weeks. Now, only one old keeper pottered about the place, more for the look of the thing than anything else, and to see that any occasional guest who turned up got a shot at something, if his inclination ran that way. The present squire was not interested, he preferred London or foreign parts.

A gamekeeper's job being impossible John had another ambition, equally hard to fulfil it seemed. Every now and then, a great shire-horse came round our way. The man who led him was smart in bedford cord breeches and drab gaiters, well-cut coat and check cap; a hunting cravat round his neck and a crop in his hand. He led his proud horse as proudly. The stallion was a king among his kind. His deep, chestnut-coloured coat, rich and shining; the white blaze on his forehead and white fetlocks, irreproachable in their spotlessness. The tight bearing rein was scarcely needed to keep that lordly neck in its curve, edged as it was with its plaited mane interwoven with ribbons of many colours. The stallion bore on his withers a neatly rolled horse blanket, and round his great middle was a broad webbing belt of red, white and blue, holding in its place on his back a square pad of felt with a gold monogram worked in each corner. The long hair of his tail was fastened up in an intricate knot, which had coloured ribbons in and out of it. The stallion, and his leader, were a noble sight. There was a joy in all that strength and beauty that made you feel proud, even if you were not keen on horses. John was entranced. He would go along with them as they left the village, running and stumbling over the gutters in the grass verge, all eyes on that great horse, until the man got tired of him and shouted at him to go home. He could think of no higher destiny than to be the one who led that splendid beast, fed him with corn and hay, brushed his sleek hide and combed out the great banner of his tail. But the breeding stables he came from were ten miles away, and you could no more get a job there by going and asking for one than you could become prime minister by looking at the Houses of Parliament. Urged on by ambition, John sounded out the stallion man when he was having a pint outside the Pheasant one day, the leading rein slipped loosely over his arm, and the great horse standing statuesque beside him. 'No chance cock, we got all the boys we want; no chance at all,' was his answer. The man finished his beer, looked into the pot to make sure there was not a drain left, and went off without even glancing at him.

So there was no future for him except on a farm, though he would not mind that so much if he could be with animals, particularly with horses. Mother worried about him a good deal. She was afraid that he might turn poacher if he stayed on in Byfield. Not that he was likely to become the kind of beer-swilling loafer who took up poaching generally; but he might be trapped into it by his knowledge of rabbits and game, which the poachers might play upon until they got him. Once in that gang, and he would have been finished. But she need not have been anxious, really. His pleasure was not to kill, but to be in the fields alone, watching the wild things in their private lives, learning their ways and their secrets.

She worried less about me, though I think she was troubled sometimes. She had always hoped that Uncle George would take to me. He hadn't any children of his own, and it seemed the sort of thing he might do; then he could work me into the brewery as a clerk or something. But he did not seem very eager. When she hinted at it, because she could not bring herself to ask outright for a favour, even from him, he put her off, said he would keep his eyes open, but there was nothing at the moment, he would let her know first chance he saw, and that sort or thing. I wasn't sorry. London was no place for me after what I had seen of it during that week I was up there. I would not have minded living with Aunt Caroline, but I was not eager for Uncle George's shouting and bullying about. Yet I hated the thought of farm work. I knew that I wouldn't be any good at it, and even if I got a job, I should probably be too useless to be kept on for long, and then I would get the sack, and nobody else would employ me, and I would be a drag on my parents. There was not much to look to in Byfield for a boy who was no good at farm work. We went to see the Rector about it, Mother and I, on a chilly evening in late February, just as the days were beginning to get a little longer, but the result of the visit was as chilling as the evening. The Rector stood all the time, warming himself at a log fire that gave all the light there was in the room, poking it now and then with a long stick. He was afraid he could not offer much hope. Byfield House was practically closed these days. There was nothing there. He might see something in one of the papers or hear of something from a friend – if he did he would let us know. There was nothing else he could suggest, he was sorry. So it looked as if, whether I wanted to or not, I should have to follow John and work on a farm. Life seemed a depressing business, whenever I thought about it. The prospect of a life sentence to drudgery, from which I could not escape and for which I was not fitted, nagged at me remorselessly. Even John was little help. He could not see my point of view. The thought of the future was like a cold hand on my heart, but it was not there all the time. A sort of gift for seeing the pleasure in things would break through the misery at times and drown everything else.

Sometimes this pleasure rose, unaccountably, into rapture. Once, I remember, as I was coming home over the rise above the village, the houses below and the familiar fields suddenly became incredibly beautiful. They were no different to what they had been before, and yet they were different. Joy burned in them. The sun had set and the trees stood out, sketched with swift, black strokes on an orange sky. The great dome of air was swept and clean. Elation rushed up inside me, as if a barrier had suddenly given way before it. Words, half-found lines of poetry, blundered about in my mind, striving to shape themselves into some expression of this intense delight; and in the end verses came, poor, broken-backed things, but seeming at that time to be a miracle. This was my own private revelation. Nobody before had ever had such thoughts, they belonged to the secret places of the soul, and were not to be spoken of even to my brother. This was my own special wonder, and the power of it lay upon me all the way home. In general I was lonely, and might have thought myself unhappy if I had known enough about other people's lives to realise that I was any different from the rest of the world, in being poor and having no hope. But to see and feel things like this must be something special; not many other people could have so fine a thing, so life would not be entirely bleak. But it would be hard enough, there would be no escape from that. I wouldn't be beaten or frightened, till I was crazy like poor Barky, Mother and Father would see to that, but even if I managed to hold on to a job and wasn't turned off to be a burden to my parents, there would be nothing but loneliness and drudgery in the years that lay ahead.

As for the drudgery, poor people living in a village like ours could never expect to get away from it. Without money, without some small influence, what hope was there? Not one in a hundred of farm labourers ever had the chance to be anything more. Those who did manage to crawl up the ladder, for a step or two, only did so by slaving practically night and day, and lying and cheating at every opportunity. There was talk at times of smallholdings being made available, and the phrase 'three acres and a cow' was passed about, as if it was going to give the labourer a little independence some time. But Lord Postern wouldn't allow any of his farms to be cut up, and there wasn't any other land that was suitable, so the talk died out. It was hard to have any self-respect when, at any minute, a man might be given the few shillings due to him and told to clear off, and not ask for a reference because he wouldn't get one; and that meant no work, unless he could find something a long way away, and move out of the district altogether. A rough word, a back answer, might bring that at any time. Self-respect wasn't easy, yet we wanted it so much that we had to have it somehow. 'Don't crawl to nobody,' Mother would say. 'Do your work, treat the gentry with respect, because that's right, they are the gentry, but don't let them wipe their shoes on you. People won't respect you for doing that. If you can't get on by honest means, don't get on by dishonest, the Lord never gave a blessing for that,' was what she taught us, over and over again, as children, striving to put into us the creed that sustained her; a creed compounded of her own resolute independence and the church-going religion she had been brought up in. I could never make out why in novels and such things the poor were generally represented as squalid or ridiculous. My parents were poor enough, God knows, but they were neither squalid nor ridiculous. They seemed good people to me, as good as any people could be. My father had the patient courage of an animal, that bears and endures, and gives of its strength without pause and with a quiet heart, because it is aware of nothing but the immediate effort. Mother had a courage of the spirit, something finer and more capable of suffering. She not only felt the struggle of the moment but also knew the bitter injustice of the life she led, which only her religion made endurable. The world was a harsh place, but she would defy whatever it might inflict upon herself, and give what small help she could to those who were even more hardly treated than she was. For her, kindness was an act of pity to the tortured human race, which needed pity so much and got so little.

Poor as we were, nobody ever came begging to our door and went away without something, even if it was just a crust of bread if he said he was hungry, or a clean shirt, patched and repatched but still holding together, if his own had fallen to pieces. Poor old Liza Bone, teetering on the edge of starvation, with parish pay of three and sixpence a week; when she had nothing in the house, and no prospect of anything, knew where to go. She would drop in about tea time and seat herself, primly, down in Father's armchair, refusing to take off her bonnet because this was purely a social call and could be nothing else. Then she would explain, that just being out for a little walk along Brandy Hole Lane, it had suddenly come over her that she hadn't heard anything about us lately, and how were the children bless their hearts, little mites she had brought into the world, though not so little now, and all doing well she hoped? Mother, perfectly understanding why she had come, would answer her questions, and give her tea with some meat and a plateful of fried potatoes, to fill her up a bit more than her usual bread and dripping, and then send her home with something to help her out for the next day or two, even if it was only an apron full of vegetables. Barky would come in of an evening now and then, for no special reason that we could make out, and sit just inside the door, wild-eyed and furtive; not saying anything very much, but comforted in some queer way by being in our house. Father, who considered everything was right if she did it, thought, well, not that she was taken in exactly, but that she allowed people to sponge on her. 'You've no call to let them do you out of the little you've got,' he would say. 'It's the poor that must look after the poor,' was always her answer, as if it was a formula she hid behind, when her conscience reproached her for giving away what her family might very well need. She was hard to fool. I expect she knew well enough in her heart of hearts, only she would never let herself face it, that the tramps who came begging to the house, and generally seemed plump enough, were better fed than we were. 'If he's told me lies, the sin is at his door, not mine,' she would say, 'you can't see folks go hungry.' But to give to people who would take the poor things she had to offer was something deep in her nature, it satisfied some kind of urge, and gave her dignity and reassurance in her own eyes. Perhaps it bolstered up her pride, though she never made a fuss and was short with people who tried to thank her more than was demanded by ordinary good manners. It was a luxury she allowed herself, the luxury of generosity, which the poor can rarely have, but which she forced her circumstances to allow her.

Chapter 11

To go back to the autumn before Granny died. Mother and I were sorting potatoes, kneeling in front of our house in the yellow November sunshine, shelling off the dry dirt, putting the grub-eaten, half-rotten ones on one side for the pig, and bagging up the rest for winter store, when I saw the man turn in at our gate. It is all mixed up together in one impression, the raw vegetable smell of the potatoes, the feeling of harvest and plenty, the pleasure of shelling off the dry clay and finding in the pieces as they dropped the delicately smooth mould of the roots they had clung to, and the surprise of this sudden stranger. He was a little man in a new brown suit. He plodded down the garden path towards us, leaning forward in his walk, his arms hanging loosely at his side, and carrying himself like a man that has been wrenched about a lot by work that was too heavy for him. His boots were new, too, and hadn't had time to get comfortable yet; the only thing about him that wasn't new was his cap, a faded blue thing, with ear flaps that were tied on the top of his head with strings. He stopped, turned a thin, brown face towards Mother, and waited for her to speak. She looked up, stared at him for a moment, calling up the memory of him from the back of her mind, then burst out, 'Good Lord Above, it's Will! Fancy you here! Why didn't you let us know you were coming?' 'I ain't much of a one for writing,' he answered slowly. They looked at each other, appraising one another, not sure of each other. Mother hated to be caught unawares by anything important. 'All that way from Canada,' she said, 'and never let us know, so that we could meet you, and had things ready for you, a bed made up.' He looked uneasy and chilled, as if something he had counted on had failed. It was only her way, I knew that, but she ought to have been able to get ready for him properly, with a special tea, and perhaps a pony and trap from the station. 'I ain't much for writing,' he said again, 'and I made up my mind all at once like.' 'Well, come on in,' she said, getting up from among the potatoes and brushing the dirt off her apron, but with more welcome in her voice. 'Bob will be fair capped when he gets in and sees you here.' She bustled about and got him a meal, fussing because she hadn't anything better to offer him, and making him feel that it was all his fault, though she meant it for compliment. Uncle Will sat and drank his tea, pouring it into the saucer and blowing on it, uneasily; glancing round the house from time to time, and then back to his tea again, as if he was puzzled but anxious not to give offence.

But the warmth of Father's welcome ought to have made up for everything. We heard him drop his dinner basket outside, then the tin bowl rattled as he got some water to wash. Uncle Will never moved, but just put down his cup and waited. The door opened, and Father came in. He stood for a minute, struggling with his surprise, then recognition spread over his face like sunlight over a grey landscape. 'If it ain't our Will, our Will, all the way from Canada!' He wrung his brother's hand and sat down, still saying, as if it was something too big to take in all at once, 'Our Will! All the way from Canada!'

'I reckon you never thought I'd be back again, did you, Bob?' 'And here you be, all the way from Canada, Will.' They seemed to find some relief, for feelings they could not express otherwise, in this Bob and Will business. They went on tacking each other's name at the end of every sentence. 'I bet it cost you a pretty penny to come, Will.' 'It did that, Bob. But I done well for myself, in Canada. I got a farm out there, Bob!' He didn't look like a man with a farm, in his cheap, ill-fitting clothes and a general air of overwork and hardship.

He was a disappointment, this uncle from Canada. Generally I pictured him with a rifle in his hand, and a fur cap on, with a tail hanging down from it; or standing, leaning on his axe, by the stump of a vast tree that he had just cut down, like the pictures in a book I had seen called *Pioneers of the Far West*. As he settled down to stay with us for a bit, he began to wander about the countryside, revisiting places he remembered, looking up old friends, having pints of beer with them, and telling them about his farm. Every other interest and desire seemed to have been burnt out of him by the strength of that one passion. It was his pride, his boast and the proof of his importance. Once he went to see Grandmother, but he made no comment when he got back. Mother and he never seemed to hit it off. She was edgy with him, and he was shy of her. He was a slow talker, as lonely people often are, but he would tell us about his farm, sitting by the fire at night; and his delight in it loosened his tongue and cleared his fumbling thoughts, so that he almost made us see the place. It had a house of squared logs, banded with white plaster, which was warm in winter and cool in summer. There were apple trees, and a big red barn, where the cattle were housed in the cold weather, with stone walling at the bottom to keep out the frost, tall wooden sides, and a steep roof to shoot off the snow. There was a split-rail fence, snaking away across pasture that was green in the summer, beneath a blue sky, and white all the winter, with its covering of snow. Twenty years of merciless self-driving was in that farm, twenty years, that others had given to home and family and love of women, he had given to that farm; and it was home and family and women's love to him. Having it made him important. He had sustained himself by thinking of the day when he would come back to Byfield and talk about his farm, and be looked up to because of it, by all who remembered him when he was penniless. But it hadn't worked out like that. His mates would drink his beer, and pat him on the back, and say, 'Good old Will. You done well for yourself,' but they didn't understand. He bored them by harping on it too much, they got tired of listening, all except Father, so he got the full benefit of it.

Uncle Will went on proving what a great man he was. 'Best day's work I ever did, going to Canada, Bob. Look what I got. But I worked, mind you. Wasn't afraid of hard work, hadn't to be. You are on your own out there, but it pays if you have got push and go, like I had. You should have had more push, Bob.' 'I reckon I should have,' said Father, meditatively; if push was what got men farms, push was what he ought to have had. 'Now you stuck here, you were talking about getting married when I left, I recollect, but there is nothing in Byfield. Stick here, and you are as well off when you die as when you are born.' That did seem to sum up Byfield pretty well, to my way of thinking. But Mother didn't like it. 'There's worse places than Byfield,' she said, bridling. The hint that stopping at home, and getting married, had kept Father poor did not please her. 'Bob has never been the one to be afraid of hard work, now then.' She would never have her husband run down by anybody, no matter who tried it. But Uncle Will was on his subject, and wasn't to be stopped. 'Work, that's how I got my bit of money together. Work, all the hours God sent, seven days a week. And now I'm my own boss.' He just wanted to be admired, for people to tell him how clever he was. Mother, who was pretty quick in the uptake as a rule, knew that well enough, but she wouldn't give in to him; all she said was, 'Didn't you ever want a wife and children? Somebody you could leave it to when you were gone?' 'Wife! What good's a wife to me?' he answered roughly. 'I'll find somebody to leave it to, when I'm ready. I ain't dead yet.' But what Mother said must have started something in his mind because once or twice in the next day or so, in a roundabout sort of way, he talked about taking John back with him, and teaching him Canadian farming, but nothing was settled. Anyway, it looked as if we might have something from him one day.

Then he took it into his head to go off to London and visit Aunt Jane. She was their sister and married to a postman. She hadn't any children, so she worked out all her natural bossiness on her husband, a man with a big nose who talked in a cockney whine. The next thing we knew was that he had gone back to Canada. He never told us himself that he was going but got Aunt Jane to write a long, rambling letter, full of how wonderful it was of Will to have done so well in Canada, and what a pleasure it had been to have him, and how much she would miss him; all jumbled up in a queer sort of way, so that Mother said it sounded as if she was ashamed of something. She wasn't very happy about the way she had treated Uncle Will herself; not that she said much, except once or twice, when she was sitting looking at the fire in the evening, it came out. 'He oughtn't to have jumped on us like that. He should have let us know that he was coming then we'd have been ready for him.' When Grandmother died, Uncle Will sent five pounds towards the funeral, and Mother wrote and told him all about it, but he didn't answer, any more than he did when she wrote at Christmas time; but we didn't take any notice of that because, like Father, he wasn't much of a writer. We heard no more about him till we got the lawyer's letter, my last winter at school.

The postman came up the garden path with it in his hand. He knew it wasn't from Ellen or anybody like that. This one had a typed address on a long, blue, expensive-looking envelope. 'Letter for you, Mrs Hillyer. A bit out of the way, too, I fancy. It'll be from a lawyer, I bet a penny. It's got a lawyer's name on the back.' 'Lawyers! God bless my soul, what do we want with lawyers?' said Mother, flustered. She wiped her wet hands on her apron before she took the letter, turned it over and over, and read the address; it had Father's name on it, but that didn't make any difference. 'Well, I must be getting on,' said the postman, without much conviction, shifting the strap of his bag on his shoulder to give him another second or two, in the hope that he would see the letter opened. But she was not going to do that while he was there. As it was he had a nice little bit of gossip to take on his round. 'Here you are, Mrs Waker, letter from your Mary. You know Bob Hillyer's, down in Brandy Hole Lane? I took a lawyer's letter there just now. Great big envelope, with a London postmark. What do you reckon that could be about now?' 'Well, fancy that! A lawyer's letter! Well I say! It'll be about his folks in London I expect. I know he's got some there. You are sure it was for Bob Hillyer? Because Lizzie Hillyer's got a brother up there. Well-to-do too, so they tell me.' 'No, Mrs Waker, it was for Bob. There it was, on the envelope, Mr Robert Hillyer and in this new-fashioned typewriting too.' Everybody on Billy Grove's round had to be told the news, so that by afternoon all the people in Byfield knew that we had got a lawyer's letter from London, and wondered a great deal about what was in it.

There wasn't very much of it, only five or six lines, but it was important. It said, in a stiff, lawyer's way, that Uncle Will was dead; he had died in a Toronto hospital, and they wanted to see Father at their office about it, but they did not seem in much of a hurry as the day they mentioned wasn't till about three weeks' time. We had got to wait till then to find out what it really meant. 'So our Will is dead, is he?' said Father slowly when he heard the news, his mind moving heavily round its implications. 'And he were set up too about that farm of his, wasn't he? It's a fine place to all accounts, and he worked hard for it. It were a rare pleasure to him to talk about it. But he were a young man! Younger than me! He oughtn't to have had to leave it as quick as that.' He sat down slowly, and ate his meal in a troubled mood. In his deliberate way he turned over in his mind the mystery of it all. It was an astonishing thing for Will to do, to go to Canada, to cut himself off from his folks like that, and risk that far away, unknown place by himself. Other people had gone there and nothing had ever been heard of them again. They had dropped out like the dead. But Will had come back rich! Still more astonishing! The first in the family with money! And he wanted people to tell him how well he had done. It didn't seem much to want. Things hadn't been right when Will was here, he didn't know why. But he had been welcome, he knew that. Nobody in the family had ever had a farm of his own before. But Will had got one, slaved night and day for it. They ought to have told him how well he had done. Will always liked a bit of praise. And now he was dead. And a young man too, as people went. What good had it done him? Father ate his meal slowly, his stumbling thoughts dropping from him in broken phrases, as his simple mind struggled with life and death, and the futility of man's endeavour. The rest of us just said yes, or nodded now and again. It was best to let him talk.

But it was all too difficult for him to grapple with for long. Bit by bit the trouble left him, and he slipped back into his old placidity. When he was sitting by the fire, with his pipe going well and his slippers on, something else struck him. 'Do you think we shall come in for anything?' he asked Mother tentatively. It was what John and I had both been thinking, but we hadn't liked to say anything. 'That depends,' she answered, putting in the next few stitches very carefully, so as not to give herself away. 'He didn't say he had made any will did he?' Father thought a minute, then said, 'There is only Jane and me now. It might come to a tidy bit.' He puffed his pipe and faced up to possible riches. 'It all depends on what farms are worth out there,' Mother added. 'There is a lot of land in Canada, so they say. Farms can't sell out there like they do here.' He thought that over for a bit. In spite of all that Uncle Will had said, his notion of a farm was what he had always known – four or five hundred acres of rich land, neatly divided by green hedges, with a comfortable old house and a farmyard belonging to it. 'A farm is worth good money wherever it is, I should say,' he answered, refusing to be impressed by Mother's hesitations.

She was aggravating! She never would let herself go, and be hopeful about anything. Always she was cautious about believing that luck might come our way. But who else was there to have the money, except Father and Aunt Jane? It was plain enough. There was no risk about it, how could there be? Perhaps, inside her, she wanted to believe that we were going to be lucky as much as we did, but she was afraid for us as much as for herself. To build up hopes, and then have them smashed was more than she could face. What reason had life ever given her for thinking that good might come? She had to save us, and herself, from the bitterness of disappointment, so it was wisest to crush down all expectation of better things, even though a faint hope that they might come to pass after all still lingered. So she kept buttoned up, and gave dry answers, when the rest of us talked big about the future. Father just sunned himself in it. 'We'll have a bit of land of our own when we get that money. I'll work for myself for a change.' That was what every farm labourer dreamed of, though the chance of it happening was like the chance of swimming the Channel, not impossible, but highly unlikely. 'I'll believe that when I see it,' was Mother's comment. 'It would be something for our John to look to,' said Father, knowing that she was worried about him, and thinking that she might unbend at that prospect. 'And Dick can go to the Grammar School, if he wants to,' he added, bolder still. But all he had for encouragement was, 'We'll spend that money when we have got it.'

The prospect of going to the Grammar School was like life for the dead. All thought of it had disappeared out of my mind. There was nothing ahead but drudgery on a farm, and even if I managed to resign myself to that, I was certain that I would never be any good at it. I did not understand animals as John did, and the heavy slavery of all the rest, blanketing the mind, dulling the senses and reducing a man to a weight-lifting, slogging lump of obtuse muscle, was dreadful to think of. But with books I could be happy. The Grammar School, if I could go there on tolerable terms, was like a break in a prison wall. Uncle Will, who was going to make all that possible, seemed to have the right ideas, and I wished that I had liked him a bit more when he was over here.

All the village knew that we were going to come into money. Billy Grove's tale about the lawyer's letter had started them off; and, remembering how Uncle Will had talked, they were pretty sure that we were in for a good thing. John and I were told, times enough, not to let people know that Father was to go up to London. 'People', Mother said, 'would find that out fast enough without us telling them.' And they certainly did find out. Father vowed that he 'knew better than to spread his concerns all over the shop, like some folks would do'; but he was a bit shamefaced about it, and the village was definitely a winner this time at the business of finding out what was in the wind, because they knew when and where he was going and had made up their minds to within a pound or two what he would get.

That stretch of three weeks was long in going. We got a letter from Aunt Jane in the middle of it, one of her long, rambling sort that was difficult to make head or tail of; all about poor Will being cut off in his prime, when he was so happy, and had worked so hard, and done so well; and would Father go to her house first, when he got to London, so that they could go to the lawyer's office together, because it was important for them both to be there at the same time. We got up at six o'clock in the morning to see Father off, the train went at half-past seven, and it was a good five-mile walk to the station. He had his black coat on, the one he had been married in, and kept for funerals ever since; but he had borrowed a pair of black trousers to go with it, because the check ones he had at his wedding wouldn't look right in London nowadays; and he had trimmed his moustache, and brushed his hair with water to make it lie flat. We felt that he was a credit to us, and the lawyer would see at once that he was a man who deserved to come into money. Mother gave him the price of his railway ticket and half a crown out of the rent money, so that he would have something in his pocket if he wanted it. When we got the legacy it could be put back. She did not say much, but it was easy to see that she wished she knew more about what was going to happen in that lawyer's office, so that she could tell him what to do, but we didn't know anything except what was in the letter.

It was a long day. The time at school dragged by. Outside, there was nothing to do that was of any interest, to take the mind off wondering and guessing what was going on in London, and when Father would be back with the news. It was a day all by itself, a day standing between two lives, because tomorrow I might be quite different from today, a boy who was going to the Grammar School and whose parents had money. I would have a bicycle, and flash along the summer roads on it, and I would have a cap with an enamel badge on the front – a little blue and gold shield – and everybody would know that I went to the Grammar School and was a clever chap and would have a good job one day. I was so full of it that I had to talk to somebody about it, but there was only Mother, and she shut me up fast enough. 'You haven't got there yet. Talk about what you are going to do when you know you are going to do it. Wait till your Father comes back.'

So we waited. We did not expect him back until after dark because, with what he had to do at that office, he would not be able to catch the twelve o'clock train, and then there would be nothing that would get him in till night. But something might happen. The lawyer might send him to the station in a cab, so that he might get the twelve o'clock after all. Even if he didn't, he might pick up a ride with somebody, and not have to walk home, and so be back that much sooner. When you came into money, and luck was with you like that, you could expect things to go your way. But it might work out opposite. There might be so many important things to do that he would not be able to get back at all, then he would have to spend the night at Aunt Jane's and send us a telegram. Bottled up, just sitting there, not allowed to say what was in your mind, the hands on the tin clock hardly seemed to move. He was not on the early train, for certain; if he had he would have been here by now. Mother had just said that it looked as if he was going to stop the night when he came in. It was not a time for anybody to speak until he did. He hung up his hat and stick, and dropped into his armchair, looking tired. His silence seemed to hit us, but he was tired, only tired, after a day like that he would be tired. Mother took his supper out of the oven and put it in front of him. He seemed to be waiting for her to speak, but she didn't say anything. At last he said, as if it was somehow his fault, 'He's left it all to Jane.' 'He has, has he,' said Mother, her voice hard, her face set. 'I thought as much when I see you come in.' 'It seems she got him to make his will that time he was over here, and was up in London so much,' he went on, getting it all out now he had started.

Everything collapsed, swallowed up in one engulfing despair. The Grammar School, the land of our own, the bright future, all that we had hoped for, smashed to bits and falling on us like a house struck by lightning. There was nothing good in the world, nothing to believe in, nothing to hope for, nothing to be trusted. We were poor, we always had been, we always should be, we were that sort of people, and there was no way out of it. Father put his hand into his pocket and took out two little packets, and gave one to me and one to John. I didn't open mine, I knew it had a book in it. John unwrapped his, and found a thick piece of catapult elastic. They were to comfort us for the Grammar School and the farm. 'They paid my fare, and Jane gave me five pounds,' he said, a little more cheerfully. Unfolding his old fustian purse, he took out some silver, and a five-pound note, smoothed out the note and laid it in front of Mother. She let it be there. 'What did they want, dragging you up to London, just to tell you there was nothing for you?' she asked bitterly. 'I had to swear to our Jane being Will's sister. It seems them lawyers don't trust nobody.' His voice rose in indignation. It was safer to be angry about the lawyers than about the money; it wouldn't burn you and break you like the other would. 'Who is there to trust?' she answered dully. I could guess what she was thinking. Had Jane worked to get us out of the will, or had it been partly her own fault? If she had got on better with him, when he was over here, would things have been different? There was no telling. All we could be sure of was that we hadn't got anything, and wouldn't have anything.

Neither John nor I made a remark. There was nothing to say. Even when we went to bed and were by ourselves, we were still silent. Each of us had his own kind of heartbreak, and mixed up with it was a sort of anger with ourselves, that we had ever been fools enough to dream our separate dreams. We had been miserable before, and we had learned the hard way that misery is best kept to oneself, everybody has enough of their own. We heard Mother and Father come up to bed a little while after, and they were not talking much either. The next day it was the same as it always had been, except for people fishing about, in a humbugging kind of way, to see if they could find out what had happened. But they didn't get much change out of us.

Chapter 12

The only thing different which happened that spring was the way Barky Britnell took to behaving. He would stand at his cabin door, these lengthening evenings, and shout at people; it was not words of any sort, just unintelligible stuff. It looked as if the prison weight of his loneliness was getting too much for him, and he had to break out of it in some way. But he still couldn't bring himself to face people. If anybody he shouted at were to stop and go towards him, he would scuttle inside and shut the battered old door, and watch from behind the scrap of curtain until they went away, and then start all over again. Everybody in the village said that he was getting madder than ever, and that he would do himself or somebody a mischief one of these days, and that the Rector ought to get him sent to the workhouse. Johnson, the man Barky worked for, was very angry about that. He said Barky was no madder than he had ever been, and if that damned interfering old parson tried to get him sent away he'd soon put a stop to that game. But everybody knew why he said it. He wouldn't get anybody else to do a man's work for boy's wages; but they knew, just as well, that if the Rector decided to do something about it Johnson wouldn't stand a chance. He was not the man to put up with nonsense from anybody if he thought that what he was doing was right. We could never make out why he didn't make Johnson pay Barky better, but he was a funny man in some ways, and perhaps he thought it wasn't the sort of thing he could do much about. Mother took to going up once or twice a week, to see that the mad old man had enough to eat and wasn't in a worse mess than usual. If he was in one of his rages, she could generally quiet him down. 'I'd have him here with us,' she said to Father, 'if only we had somewhere to put him. Barky is all right, if people treat him right.' 'But there ain't anywhere,' said Father, as if he was meditating the problem, but sounding relieved, nonetheless, that there was no solution to it.

Spring came fully on and gave us other things to talk about. You could generally tell what would be in people's minds by the time of year. With so little that was new in our lives, we were forced to find variety in small things, to live minutely. The level of water in a ditch compared with this time last year, the budding of a tree that was earlier than usual, the preferences of animals that made them choose one side of a field rather than another at any particular time; the coming of the blossom, the thickness of the foliage, the height of the grass as against what might be expected at the time of year, and a hundred other changes so small that only those who minutely observed familiar things every day could notice any difference, were the staple of our conversation. Silly people, who laughed at country folk for being slow, didn't know what they were talking about. A countryman in a town was out of his element, his senses were bludgeoned and dazed with too much variety, with objects too large and too swiftly changing, that choked his comprehension. He was like a man who has looked through a microscope for a long time, and then takes his eye away from it, the proportion of everything has changed too suddenly. But in his own place he was quick to see, and interpret, every minute difference in the world around him.

Most of what happened had to do with the slow changes of the seasons, so gradual in their development that each seemed to fuse with the other. On a cold day in February, when everything looked at its bleakest, if you happened accidentally to kick on one side a rotten lump of last year's leaves, you would find some yellow shoots springing up beneath them, to show that life was coming back to its own again. Slowly, the evenings got lighter, and the mornings. The March winds were cold, but they dried up the mud that was ankle-deep in the farm gateways, and dispersed the clinging damp which made cold seem so much colder. Lambing time was over, and everybody was glad of that because it meant being up all hours of the night with the ewes. Children stayed out to play after school, and had to be fetched in by their mothers, who were glad of an excuse to walk up as far as the top green after being in all the winter evenings. Everybody's spirits rose, as the sap rose in the trees. The first daffodils came out, putting little touches of living yellow into the dead cottage gardens; and women who had half an hour to spare of an afternoon began to dig about among the roots of the flowers with broken knives, so that the primroses would show up nicely against the black soil, and everything look tidy for the spring. The evenings were lengthening out a good deal, and the men were hard at work digging, ready for the vegetables. Wives, if they were in a companionable mood, would stand without coat or hat, watching them, meditatively scratching their elbows and offering little bits of advice about what ought to go here, or over there, when the plants were ready to be set out.

Then, before you knew it, Easter had come, and Easter is the threshold of summer. Easter was the day for new clothes. You knew which families in the village were respectable and provident because they were the ones who made their children save the Randall clothes for Easter Sunday. The feckless types would let the children put them on the minute they got them, so that they were practically knocked to pieces before Easter. The church was a sight to see, because Mrs Du Cane sent down dozens of flowering plants from her conservatory in pots and had them stacked in great banks of colour on either side of the altar. People even came from as far away as Billington to look at them, so that the church was always packed on Easter Day. And there were cheerful hymns to sing, and the choir's surplices were stiff and white, with starch and recent washing, and the polished brass caught and reflected the different lights so that it seemed alive. And with all this delight of sight and sound there was the glory of a new suit, and new boots, even though they had not yet shaped themselves so as to be comfortable, but made you feel as if you were done up in a parcel. It was the last time I would get the Randall clothes, because by next winter I would be at work, and not eligible. I would have liked time to stand still that spring, so that I could go on like that for ever, but it wouldn't, and I would have to leave school in June. I was going to work at Johnson's. Father had tried to get me a job with him at Bratton's, but there wasn't anything there, and I had to take what I could get.

There were some signs about, just then, that times might change. Already old people were getting Lloyd George's money – five shillings a week, instead of three and six parish pay – and nobody to bow and scrape to when you drew it; but just go along to Selina Vear's with your book, and there it was, waiting for you. People up top were wanting to do something for the villages at last. They started sending lecturers round, and some of them were women, which was even more extraordinary. One of them, quite a good-looking young woman too, with nice clothes, came to Byfield and had an afternoon meeting in the parish room, with a free cup of tea, and talked about lace-making. A lot of it used to be done in our parts at one time, now only old Selina knew the way of it. She used to sit in her shop, a fat old woman in a black dress stuck all over the front with pins, with a bulging black silk pillow on her knees; her pudgy hands throwing the bobbins over one another with incredible speed, and producing long strips of the delicate lace which had made our countryside famous at one time. But the women were not interested in lace-making any more, so they drank the tea, and said, 'Yes, ma'am' and 'No, ma'am' primly to the lady lecturer, and did nothing else about it. So another came, and this one talked about straw-plaiting. There had been a time when Byfield had been famous for that, too. Mother had spent many hours doing it when she was a girl; so had all the rest of the women of her age, and every one of them hated the thought of the monotonous, ill-paid labour. A good many of the houses still had the little mangle-like machine fastened to the back of the living-room door, which had been used to flatten out the many yards of completed plait, which sold for a few pence to the hat makers. Nobody at the meeting wanted to bring those worm-eaten old rollers into use again. So they drank the cup of tea, and said 'Yes, ma'am' and 'No, ma'am' primly to the lady lecturer, and did nothing about it. The movement for reviving rural industries was not succeeding very well among us. The common opinion in the village was that if the County Council and people like that wanted to do us a good turn, their best thing would be to get the men more wages.

Then the man came with the van. That was the most extraordinary thing of all. He was there when we went into school in the morning, so he must have started early from wherever he came from, to arrive by that time. Already he had begun setting up his things on the top green, as if he was some sort of showman. The van was a big green affair like a caravan, drawn by two horses that were turned out to graze at the moment, their traces looped up on their backs. They seemed fairly used to it, for they were moving about gently, side by side, nibbling at the grass. The van had little doors that lifted up on hinges all round it, and one big door at the back, big enough to get in by, with a brass knob on it. Nobody had ever seen anything like it before, it was a marvellous van, a van to be studied in all its details. The man who was with it was a wiry little person, who went about his work quickly and methodically, as if it was something that he did every day of his life. When he had blocked all the wheels, and made sure that everything was right, he took his horses off to the Pheasant and it was time for us to go to school. He was there again when we came out, on the top of the van this time, throwing down some poles and a big net made of very fine mesh, which he put up all round the van and all over it; keeping us running about, bringing him the things he needed. We didn't mind, because we wanted to find out what he was up to. When he had got the net up, and had fussed all over it to make sure that everything was right, he opened each of the little doors, and slowly, cautiously, bees began to come out; a few at a time, and then an eager stream of them, as their scouts found the heavy heads of red clover, warm and sweet in the sun. The man didn't seem to mind the bees buzzing all around him. He came out from under the net, carefully fastened the opening, and went back to the Pheasant again. We still couldn't make out what it was all about. What was he doing with a van-load of bees on our top green? So we tagged off behind him, and let ourselves in for more work; because he came out with a bundle of handbills, and told us to take one to every house in the parish, and he might give us a penny later on. We hadn't much faith in that penny, but we took the bills, because we wanted to see what was in them; they were all about a meeting that was to be up by the van that night, at seven o'clock.

There was a good turn-up, when the time came, because nobody had ever known a meeting of that sort before, and there wasn't much doing in the gardens between seasons to keep them away. Even Mrs Blore was there, standing up at the front, and listening to the man as if she really wanted to know what he was saying. Nobody else cared very much, but it was a meeting and something different, so they were glad to be there. There were big coloured pictures of bees and flowers hung up all round the netting, to show what they were like, and how they got their honey; it was as good as a wild beast show at a fair. The man put on a big hat, with gauze hanging down all round it, and went under the netting; explaining that the hat was not necessary for him, because the bees wouldn't sting him anyway, but he was just doing it to show us. If anybody was afraid of bees they could wear something like that, and be safe; but bees wouldn't sting if they were handled without haste and without fear. Then he took the hat off and let the bees crawl all over him, to show that there was nothing to be afraid of. It was a wonder! There he stood, in a sort of cloud, thousands of lightly moving wings which settled and rose and filled the air around him with an undulating mass; now dense, now thinned out, as if it was their purpose sometimes to hide and sometimes to reveal the ecstatic mystery they centred round. It wasn't human! Anybody else who did that would be stung to death. It didn't help him any. People were suspicious of a fellow who could do that.

He opened some more little doors in the van and let us look right into the hives inside, with bees crawling all over the glass, and in and out of their combs, and told us that these were patent hives that were a lot better than the old-fashioned sort, and didn't waste the honey, which was a silly thing to do because it was worth good money. He said that everybody ought to keep bees, because you could make a lot out of them, selling honey to the shops at a good price, but nobody was interested except Mrs Blore who, of course, would want to try her hand at it. Nobody kept bees in Byfield except Johnny Batson, who had a few skeps standing on a rotten bench under his apple trees. People used to buy honey off him, for sore throats and things like that, but you had to fetch it in a mug, and it generally had bits of comb in it. Bees were 'unked'* things, nobody wanted to fool about with them.

When the bee man had finished talking he gave out some little books and said that if anybody wanted to know anything more his address was at the town hall in Billington and he would answer enquiries by post at any time; then he shut up the little doors, because the sun was down now and the bees were all inside, and went off to the Pheasant for his supper. A wild sort of thought sprang up in me. I might keep bees. I could do it, if everything else failed. Suppose I got the sack, because I was hopeless, and nobody else would give me any work, and I had to live on my parents, perhaps I needn't be such a loss to them. I could get the bees from somewhere, and keep them in our garden, and the man said there was money in it. It was a chance, a faint kind of possibility, just enough to offer a pin-point of hope, because I was certain that I should be no good at farm work, and there was nothing else.

* Strange, uncanny

Chapter 13

But in fact, when I did start work, it wasn't at all bad. Like so many things that you are frightened of and dread doing, it turned out to be easier at first than it seemed as if it would be. It was early July, and haymaking was just beginning. Summer is always a good time, it is better both outdoors and in. The house smells fresher when you can have the doors open all day, and a handful of sticks, which is all you need to boil the kettle, is a more cheerful sort of fire to look at than a shovel-ful of wet slack, smouldering and smoking away; which is what you have generally got in the grate in wintertime. I was to start on Monday morning, and all that Sunday the thought of it loomed heavy and ominous. Fear is where you find it, and is as big as you make it, and for me it lay just ahead, and was very big indeed. My first job was to catch the horses, which were wanted for mowing, and take them to the field, where the carter was waiting for them. He was a foul-tempered man, and I was pretty sure that something would go wrong and get me into trouble with him. But the horses behaved like lambs. They had been worked hard for the past week, and that had taken some of the life out of them I expect; anyway, they came gently along, just dragging on their halters enough to show that they were not over-anxious to start work. 'So you got 'em then,' Spicer growled. 'Your John would have had 'em here in half the time,' but that didn't bother me, because I knew he couldn't have done.

After that it was easy. My job was to keep lively, and bring him whatever he wanted – he was too lordly to get off the machine and fetch anything himself – and when I wasn't bringing him the beer jar, or some string, or the file, or anything else he wanted, to rake away the thick swathe where it hindered turning; or to lift up the long grass where the foxes at play, or some trick of the wind, had laid it too flat for the chattering blade of the mowing machine to get beneath it. Over all that first day lay a vast sense of relief. Fear ebbed away. The air was still, and the sun shone. It was pleasant to be in my shirt sleeves, pleasant to be earning something, pleasant to listen to the steady, purposeful clatter of the machine as it made its large circuit round the field, its loose, metallic rattle loud near at hand, muted into a soft drone by the distance, and then loud again, as it turned to come back. A couple of wood pigeons, up in the thick foliage of an elm tree, were keeping up a conversation between themselves with rich, throaty calls; stopping for a moment, and on their guard while the mowing machine was beneath them, but back again to the topic which absorbed them as the noise moved away. The cut grass itself, lying in thick swathes, was a wonder and delight; heavy and pale at the butts, tapering away into thin, green spears and an infinite variety of finely fretted grass heads, shaped as beautifully as wrought jewels, and as graceful in their fall as snowflakes. Lines, whole verses, formed themselves in my head as I worked. They rhymed and scanned, so I thought them poetry and was happy. We had a break at ten o'clock. Spicer sat himself down on a heap of grass, with his back to me, and ate bread and bacon in sullen gloom. He took no notice of my being there, and I was glad enough to be let alone. The morning went smoothly by. Nobody came near us, nothing changed, except that the patch of unmown grass grew smaller and smaller until, when we stopped cutting for the day, at twelve o'clock, it stood up like a pattern of green velvet on a broad brown cloth. The horses, when their traces were unhooked, stood with their heads drooping, idly swishing away with their long tails the more intrusive flies, but too tired to bother over much; just dozing while we got our things together, and Spicer covered up the mowing-machine blade with armfuls of grass, to keep it from rusting in the next night's dew.

My first morning's work was over. I was not just pleased that I had escaped trouble, I was happy in a new experience, something had been added to the delight of life. However it went on, the first few hours of earning a living had been pure pleasure. The afternoon was different, but easy enough. All the machines had to be brought out into the fields, oiled and got ready. Everybody was cheerful, because the weather was good and hay-making was beginning. It was a good day, all of it, but the morning was something special.

When we really got started the work was long and hard. Mowing from seven till ten, then a break for a bite and a drink of beer, and to turn the horses loose for a rest until they were wanted again. There was little overtime money, but some free beer to keep the men happy. It was thin, sour stuff, but we drank it; swishing the last drain round in our tin pots and saying that it was 'belly-ache mixture', 'water the brewer's men washed their aprons in.' If the jar went back to the farmhouse too often for a refill, sharp words were said about some people never being satisfied. Haymaking was hard work, but everybody was together, and that made for chaff and jokes which helped the day along; but it seemed to go on for ever, limited only by what the horses could stand, the men didn't matter.

When the mowing stopped and the horses were turned out to graze, everybody set to work to turn over yesterday's cutting. Men and boys moved in a line, each a step or two behind the other, backwards and forwards across the field at a quick walk, turning the swathe, with a deft touch of the rake, in an unbroken ribbon. It was hard to keep up at first, but as the knack grew and the movements became familiar, there was something soothing in it. All day there were the changing scents of the hayfield. The raw smell of the fresh grass in the morning, the honey smell of clover, the earthy dampness of the underside as the rakes exposed the long lines of drying grass to the sun, the sweet, dry perfume of the hay that was loaded in the evening; all of it unique, primeval, satisfying. There was the pleasure of working in company, the gossip as the haymakers moved across the field at the pace set by the leader; making it a point of honour that there was not a yard different in the interval that separated them when they finished to that which lay between them when they started. A gulp of cold tea for the boys, of beer, if there was any, for the men, a moment's breather at the turn round, and we were off again. Just a quick glance, to rest the eyes, at the distant fields, which never looked so peaceful as in haytime, or the cattle so lazy and contented, and then down at the rake again, and the steady wave of turning grass that fell from it.

The dinner-hour break was something to look forward to, and bliss when it came. A nice, full sensation, when the bread and meat and the cold vegetables out of a tin dish were all gone; and then, while the men dropped asleep, to lie on one's back and dream, relaxed, awake. The sky is a great place for losing yourself in, for forgetting monotonous labour, plodding ways and the narrowness of life. All that space, all that brightness! The occasional cloud, white, like stray tufts of clean wool, only full of slow-moving patterns, as if each cloud was a living thing with some evolution proceeding within itself. And beyond it, depth on depth, and still more depth, that seemed to draw you into it, light and free, and loose from everything. Then, tired of lying that way, to turn over on to a comfortable full belly and see a world in reverse – the quick, scurrying, secret life that goes on at the grass-roots, and from being lost in size and depth to be lost in smallness. There was never much talk at dinner-time. As soon as the men had swallowed their food they dropped off to sleep. In haytime you had to take what rest you could get.

By two or three o'clock, if the weather was good, there was new hay to carry. The horses were brought in and harnessed up. The men split up into their teams; two to pitch, and one to load, with a boy at the horse's head to lead, and take the full cart to the rickyard, and bring it back when it was empty. Everything went according to an immemorial plan, a timeless rhythm. Mile after mile, backwards and forwards, plodding on. Weariness passed into a daze, heavy boots felt like lumps of lead, arms and legs like bits of limp string. Too stupid with tiredness to feel relief, we pushed the last forks full of hay into the hopper, and left them to creak their way up the elevator on to the stack. The old horse, that went round and round all day to keep the machinery going, got slower and slower; and needed more shouts, and more stick, to keep him moving at all. The weary animal in the cart shafts drooped, and fell asleep. On a busy day, when there was a warm sun and a gentle wind, so that the hay made quickly and all yesterday's mowing was fit to carry, the church clock would be striking ten before the jerky racket of the elevator was still, the sheet pulled over the stack in case of rain, and the horses turned out for the night, the shape of the harness they had worn all day still outlined on their dark bodies with the white of dried sweat. We were glad enough then to fling our rush dinner baskets over our shoulders, the empty tea can rattling about in it as we walked, and trudge off home; with feet sore and swollen from being about on them all day, the palms of the hands stiff and shiny from the long friction of rake handles and pitchforks; yet somehow not dissatisfied because work was over for another day, and it was summertime.

Haymaking went on longer than usual that year, for it was a good season. The wet spring had brought plenty of grass, and the weather turned just in time to dry it well, and quickly, as it should be dried. Hay sold for a good price in the hunting stables round about, and Johnson wanted to make all he could, so he kept us at it. For weeks I never opened a book, and began to sink into that sullen stupidity I guessed would come; numbed in mind and body by killing tiredness. Every night I dropped asleep over my supper, and then woke up just enough to crawl upstairs and fall into bed. And it went on and on, and seemed to have no end. Sunday was the only break, and then the racked body cried out to be let alone for an hour or two, so that the muscles could loosen, the blood flow more easily, and the mind have rest from driving the weary flesh. A black depression spread over me. 'This is what it is going to be from now on,' I thought. 'What else can it be? Lifting, hauling, shoving, trudging about from day to day, nothing else through all the years, until I am old and crippled with rheumatism, and then there will be a few shillings a week to keep me from dying of starvation too soon. No other future but that! What was the use? Why not give up thinking of anything different? Accept it. Be a lump, and done with it.' But life got a bit more normal after a time. Hours were shorter when the haymaking was finished, there was less rush, and the work grew less exhausting as the body toughened up. I began to look for books again, as the addict seeks his drug. Only it was hard to find any. Mrs Blore had been my standby, but she had nothing now that I had not read except books about gardening and botany, and some in French. I was half a mind to ask her if she would teach me French, but I thought she might not take it very well, and I did not want to risk being stopped from going to her house.

But I had some money of my own now, not much, a shilling a week out of the five I earned, but you could do a lot with a shilling. Boys who hadn't got a girl generally went to Billington on Saturday nights, and blued their money on sweets from the stalls in the market, or having a go at the hoopla, or the shooting gallery, where there was a woman in a cowboy dress who loaded the guns, or even lashing out with half pints of beer, or shandy gaff, filling in the time by standing about and passing remarks at the girls. Sex was no titillating mystery to a country boy, bred up among animals, and with people who took bodily functions naturally enough. The whole cycle of procreation, and birth and life and death, was going on openly all around him. But this sort of cart-horse courtship seemed boring stuff, and these clumsy girls too silly to bother with. Pushing against one, as she was buying something at a stall, or pulling her hair when she wasn't looking, or smacking her bottom, was not for me. Too many Victorian novels had given me romantic notions about falling in love, and I wanted something better than this. But the racket of the market on a Saturday night was exciting. Butchers, shouting their heads off trying to get rid of the last cheap scraps of doubtful meat, yelled against the man with the crockery and the five-shilling watches, who was knocking one on the board in front of him to show how strong it was, and offering one, absolutely free, cup and saucer with every watch sold; because he only had two dozen left, and his boss would give him the sack if he took any of them back to London. The noise, the naphtha flares, the cheerful people made you feel alive.

Up at the top end of the market there was not much light and hardly anybody about. There looked to be something like a heap of furniture up there. For half a minute destiny balanced me in its hand, wondering whether to throw me away or encourage me to go on. I strolled up that way. It was furniture, stacked up in a sort of hollow square; old cupboards, bedsteads, tables and chairs, heaped together with an empty space in the middle. There was not much point in going any further; the lights and the people were at the other end of the market. Still, I might as well go on to the top, and then wander back. A man and a woman came out from among the furniture, carrying an ancient basket chair. Out in the light the woman poked it about, turned it upside down, examined it all over, and then planted it firmly on the cobbles and stepped back to see if it stood straight. The man said, 'Yes, ma'am, there it is, and if you can find a better chair than that for eighteen pence in this market, or in any other, I'll give it you, that's what I'll do, I'll give it you.' The woman answered anxiously, 'Yes, but Grandad is a big man, and it's no use buying anything that won't stand up to his weight. Will it stand up to his weight? That's the trouble.' She stood looking at it, her head on one side and her purse in her hand, wondering if it would stand up to Grandad's weight. In the alcove, among the furniture, there were books! Books in bundles tied up with string, books in heaps among the table legs, stuffed into shelves, lying all over the place! I slipped through the opening. The man and the woman were hard at it – if they had not been I might not have had the pluck, because I had never been in any shop other than Selina Vear's by myself before. There was a board, propped up on a broken-legged sofa, with 'Books 3d.' scrawled on it in white paint. I grabbed one – it was a dingy Shelley – and pushed the coppers into the man's hand. He never looked at me, or at what I had got: the woman was on the point of deciding, and needed all his attention.

He just said 'Thanks, chum' and I was off.

But I was back again the next week, and making a bee-line for the furniture place. It was in the covered part of the market, and had a board running all along the top of it with 'George Stubbs. Second-hand furniture Bought and Sold' on it. The board, with its post at each end, looked as if it was a sort of tie to hold the battered heap of junk together. George Stubbs himself was inside, without a customer this time, and titivating up something with a pot of stain. He was a thin, pale-faced man, with a drooping moustache which he chewed the ends of occasionally. The dirty straw boater he had on was part of his market uniform; the other part was a stained linen apron, splashed all over with the stuff he used for freshening up the furniture. When he shut up for the night he hung the boater on the knob of a cupboard door and put on a bowler. For a casual sale he just tucked up the apron, for an important customer he took it off; at the end of the day he rolled it up and put it away under the sofa. He was always touching things up with a jam-jar full of brown stain and the stump of a brush. He never mended anything, all he did was to go over them with the stain. It took the dust and fust out of his stuff anyway.

He nodded when I went in, and dabbed away at the chest-of-drawers he was attending to, accompanying himself with a blowing noise that was almost a whistle. Here were all the books I had ever wanted! The find of a lifetime! Money no object! Mr Stubbs had only two prices, 3d. and 1/-. The shilling ones were large, on thick paper, with gaudy covers, and big pictures inside; annuals and bound numbers of art magazines, and things of that kind. They were of no use to me. All that I wanted were among the threepennies. The sheer plenty was overwhelming. A shilling would buy four, but which four? He watched me out of the corner of his eye as I turned his stock over, glancing at a bit here and there, and then putting the book back to start on another. 'You look as if you like reading them things,' he said, thinking I was not going to buy anything after all. 'Yes, I like books.' 'Well I don't. They clutter up the place, get in the way. There ain't no sale for 'em, and that's a fact.' He came over for a chat, with the brush and pot of stain in his hands. 'I've a good mind to set fire to the lot of 'em.' 'Oh, I wouldn't do that,' I said hastily. It would be too bad if he meant it, and I was robbed after all. 'Why, I should think there would be plenty of people who would want to buy books like these.' 'Not here there ain't. All they want is furniture. Furniture is what I deal in, but when you buy a lot at an auction, or just clean out somebody's house, you get all this thrown in with it. They are in the way. I ain't got the room for them, and that's the truth.' 'I'd come and sort them over for you, if you like; put them in order a bit, and straighten up the shelves, so that they didn't take up so much room.' 'Well, there might be something in that. Is that the lot you are going to have?' He looked at the books I had taken, as if it surprised him that anybody should want to spend money on them, put a bit of string round them, and handed them back. It was a set called *Half Hours with Best Authors*, in four volumes. They had been noble in their day, with leather backs and marbled covers, but the finery was scratched and dingy now, the steel engravings faded and speckled. At that moment, the all-important thing was that within the battered covers were bits and pieces from a vast range of literature, people I had always wanted to read, and others I had never heard of, but standing in the full tradition and waiting to be discovered. It is easy to talk of epochs in a life, events which are permanent and far-reaching, enough to be called rare, but this was one. The dilapidated old book opened to me the sweep and grandeur of English literature better than most professional teachers would have done. It was literature itself, not talk about literature. It made its own impact, spread the goods out in front of me, and let me make my choice. Nobody told me what I ought to like, it was just there for me to like, if I wanted to. All the great people were there, from Chaucer to Tennyson, in passages which were supposed to take half an hour to read; and there was one for every day of the year, with a gossipy little introduction to each which gave all that was needed to be in the picture. From them I learned that behind the English writers lay others, belonging to far off times and places, in the old days of Greece and Rome; and that was a fact that I had never heard of before, but something to go into, if ever the chance came along. Mr Wickens taught me to like books, when he gave out his odd collection on Friday afternoons, but Mr Stubbs had provided the beginnings of an education.

Next week I was back again, and the week after that, and every Saturday night. It was the great event, the thing to look forward to through all the days that came between. Sometimes I was lucky and got a ride; then there was longer time for turning over the stock, and straightening it a bit, and talking to Mr Stubbs. He got quite to look forward to my coming. 'Here you are again,' he would say cheerfully, 'after them books again. I never see such a chap. What do you want with all them books?' And then he would leave me to root about on my own, coming over for conversation now and then, when there were no customers about. He was a talkative man – on one subject – Robert Blatchford. 'What a young chap like you ought to do,' he said, almost as soon as I got to know him, 'is to take an interest in the future of the working classes. Now Robert Blatchford, he's got it. He's got what we want. We'll have Merrie England back again, that's what Robert Blatchford says. Merrie England! And we need it! We'll have each for all, and all for each. Everything owned by the people, everything used for the benefit of the people. Socialism is bound to come. You read Robert Blatchford, and see what he says about it.'

'Who is Robert Blatchford?'

'A chap up in Manchester, who runs a paper called *The Clarion*.' He produced that week's copy from his pocket, and read me a piece. It sounded good stuff. But I wasn't ready for it. I never heard anybody talk politics at home. When there was an election Father went along and voted Liberal. The Tory always got in, nobody else stood a chance, that was all I knew about politics. But Stubbs's talk about Blatchford seemed to have sense in it. 'Everyman his own master,' he would say. 'That's the ticket. None of these bosses working a man to death, and then throwing him away when they have done with him. Why, look at me! My chest is bad. I used to drive a horse and trap for an auctioneer. Out and about, all hours, all weathers, round at cattle markets and sales, and valuing property, and all that. One day he said to me, "George," he said, "you'll have to give it up. Your chest is weak, you can't stand it. You'll have consumption before you've done, and then where shall we be? I've no fault to find with you, you do your work all right, but you'll have to give it up. It's for your own interest." Your own interest, my foot! What he was thinking of was that if I got bad he might have to pay something. So he gave me a week's notice, just like that! Twelve years I had worked for him, and he gave me a week's notice! So I started this fiddling job. I knew what you could pick up at sales, you see, if you went the right way about it. But it isn't a living and that's a fact, a starving more like. Now Robert Blatchford wouldn't have any of that. You wouldn't be wasting the best years of your life, and then have nothing to show for it. He sees different.' Stubbs's thin, hopeless face grew keen and his moustache almost bristled at the thought of it. 'You read Robert Blatchford.' He always said the full name – Robert Blatchford – as if there was something particularly satisfying about it.

He pushed some back numbers of *The Clarion* into my hand, but I was not keen about them. I had just discovered Cowper's poetry, and carried a book of it about in my pocket. There were good bits in *The Clarion* – poetry, and articles about literature, and that sort of thing – but its politics were outside my interest at the time. Poor Cowper, with his madness and his pets and his moralising, was what I wanted, and beyond the man himself, the sweet flow of his verse. Then it was Sir Thomas Browne, and then somebody else, so that I never had time to get round to Blatchford's theories about socialism. I was splashing about in language just then, the pictures that lie hid behind words, information was less important. But Stubbs kept pushing socialism at me. 'A young chap like you ought to take an interest in the movement. We've got to get the young interested. Us old 'uns have had it. But we can see you young 'uns get a better future. You ought to be in the movement.' So I said that I would go to one of his meetings. I owed him that much.

There were four or five of them standing in a self-conscious little group by the clock tower in Billington marketplace the Sunday night I turned up. The deacon on duty outside the Baptist Chapel, a plump man with a bald head and a beard, in a black frock-coat, glowered at us from across the way. We were rather handicapped by having nothing to sing, otherwise we might have been a religious meeting. The deacon went in and shut the door, because the service inside was just starting. The market square was almost empty. Mr Stubbs went up on to the steps below the clock and began his speech, and a tall man in a very high collar, who looked like a clerk, interrupted him periodically to ask a question. They had worked this out beforehand, and considered it a very deep dodge for getting a crowd together. The idea was that passers-by would think there was a row on, and stop to listen. But they didn't, not many of them anyway. There were a few dirty boys from Clay Pit Lane, the slummy part of Billington, a few men on the way to their Sunday evening pint, and one or two respectable people who stopped for a minute on the pavement opposite, and looked disgusted, but nobody else. The boys soon found more interesting things to do, and a sociable pint can't be put off too long, so we finished in about half an hour, with no more than we started. 'A very promising meeting, Mr Topping,' said Stubbs to the tall man. 'Yes, you had them listening, you did indeed, Mr Stubbs.' I didn't go again, and in a week or two the Baptist deacon got the meeting stopped – his brother was the Town Clerk – so that let me out.

Bit by bit, by working at it for an hour or two every Saturday night, Mr Stubbs's jumble of books were dusted off, tidied up and stacked in odd places among the furniture in the best sort of order I could make. I had no more notion what their value was than he had – threepence a copy seemed all right to me. Occasionally somebody came in and bought one, but not often. The dismal-looking stall, tucked away at the dark end of the market, didn't attract customers of that sort, even if there were many in Billington, which was doubtful. John helped me put up some shelves in a corner of our bedroom, and before very long they were filled with my purchases: a great, fat, broken-backed Shakespeare among them that took up all one glorious Sunday, except for church time, in reading the famous bits. The daily plod had at least one satisfaction in it, from it came the money to buy books.

Chapter 14

There was no chance of a better job in Byfield, and no hope of getting out of it. So far as I could see nothing would happen, nothing would change. It was like settling down into a deep bed of mud, cold, gluey, isolating. When I was working about on the farm by myself it was not so bad; I could think, and dream, and imagine things, but it all had to stay shut up inside me and made the isolation more complete. Mr Stubbs, on a Saturday night, was some relief; but I wished he would sometimes talk about other things than the opinions of Robert Blatchford and the bad state of business. There was not even the old comfort of having John about, because Johnson had taken it into his head that there was money in horse-dealing and was all over the place at fairs and sales, buying and selling, and always took John with him. John could handle horses as well as a full-grown man, and was a lot cheaper. Loneliness is something that takes getting used to, and it did not come easily.

Now and again, at the weekend, I might run into some of the boys I had been with at school. 'How do Dick?' 'How do?' 'Coming with us?' 'I got something I want to do at home.' 'See you in Billington the other Saturday night, up in the market. What was you doing up in the market, Dick?' 'Having a look round.' 'Having a look round! I bet! Mucking about with them old books, more like. You going to be a parson or something?' That was meant to be wit. Everybody in the gang laughed at that. Nobody read books except parsons and schoolteachers, me being a parson or a schoolteacher was very funny. 'So long, Harry, I got to go.' 'So long, Dick.' I would move away, feeling angry and foolish; but what was the use of having a row, a fight wouldn't do any good, and in any case they would gang up on me, why give them the pleasure? Then, when I was a yard or two down the road, near enough to hear but too far away to be sure which one said it, somebody would shout, 'He's going home to read some poetry. "The boy stood on the burning deck." "Call me early mother dear."' Then the whole silly lot of them would double up at such a lovely piece of humour. Once or twice, when they really got me on the raw, I went flailing into them, and got knocked about a bit. It was wiser to keep out of their way, but it was not the less lonely all the same. But what I was most afraid of, even more than the loneliness and the dim future, was that it would all get the better of me and I would lose heart; that, bit by bit, the feelings and thoughts that made up my own special life would be swamped beneath the heavy stupidity, the animal indifference, that hemmed me in.

For those sudden exaltations that exploded around me, out of nowhere, were what I had to hang on to at all costs; and yet I could not hang on to them, for they came and went as they pleased. Sometimes it was a poem, or a piece of prose, that touched off the magic, that brought the lift of the heart that was like a fountain breaking into the sunlight. Sometimes just an ordinary thing would suddenly make itself new and marvellous. It might be no more than a bird preening itself on some isolated twig that stood out above the hedgerow against a bright sky; and all at once I would be at one with it in a world of wings, and great spaces, and freedom, and pulsing delight. At some moments the fields themselves, their contours, the light and shade across them, would fall into a pattern of shattering beauty; or it might be some casual shape, like the corner of a broken wall or a tumbled-down shed, that was transformed into wonder. Then everything quickened, and there was a feeling of unity with all the world, and mysteries made clear. It might happen with people sometimes, though not to the same extent. Suppose I happen to be walking up Brandy Hole Lane, on a summer evening, and see a fat girl painting a garden gate. Nothing extraordinary, just that. She is bending at the knees a little, to get down to it, so she bulges in different places. Suddenly I know what she feels like, laying that paint on thick and black, watching it settle down into a smooth coat, with an enjoyment that is almost sensual; and adding to the pleasure by thinking, at the same time, about what she is going to have for supper. I know, because in a way I am her, that she thinks there is nothing better than being a fat girl painting a gate on a summer evening and thinking of what she is going to have for supper. But moments like this could not be forced, they came of themselves or not at all.

At other times the imagination, roaming around in search of something to feed on, had to find it where it could. There wasn't much. The secure heart of England in which we lived had no history to speak of. But there were old buildings, and they, like old clothes, carry the stamp of their previous owners upon them. It was easy to populate the brick barns and outhouses, weathered by the centuries, with the people who had once moved in and out of them, as I was doing every day. The worn cart tracks, made by hundreds of years of coming and going, called up all those who had passed along them, and died, leaving behind no other signs of their having been alive than the marks of their going to and fro, and a sagging mound in the churchyard. And yet the feel of them was everywhere; the unspoken loving, hoping, dreaming of past generations, life indestructible, created by the dead. It poured itself out continually, this life; bubbled up in every generation, insatiable in its desires, irresistible, and yet above all things vulnerable; something that possessed people, and made them capable of entering into both pain and delight, and then left them, deserted and dirty, as a bird leaves last year's nest. Now and then time played a casual trick and kept a particular name, a particular memory, alive. We had an old wagon on the farm that stirred up a lot of sentimental notions. It was large, beautiful in its lines and workmanship. It was brought out in haytime, usually; but for the rest of the year it stood in an open shed and the hens roosted on it, fouling up its once bright yellow paint and scratching about between the old-fashioned red wheels that sloped inward from the rim to the hub. Wagons like that are not made any more. Every time anybody took it out they were pretty certain to say, 'Ah, they don't make wagons like this today.' The man who built it had his name painted in small, curly letters on the axle-tree and the date, Joseph Briggs, 1815, the very year of Waterloo.

Grandfather had met a man from that old, far-off time, so

Father said. It was one of the tales he used to tell us when we were children. There was a streak of romance in him which made this the favourite of all his stories; he always looked pleased and interested when he told it. Whenever we asked him he would begin, 'I've heard my Dad tell about a feller he see once, who had fought the French, in them old-fashioned wars with the Duke of Wellington. My Dad were a lad at the time. He was hoeing up in the Forty Acre piece. It were late that year, owing to the wet, and the weeds had got a hold. The thistles were something dreadful. Old Arnison's father had the farm then, and he wanted every hoe he could get, to have them weeds down before they choked the wheat. Well, he set on an old man off the roads, a thin old man he were, I remember my Dad saying, with his hair long, down to his shoulders. He asked for a bit of a job, and Arnison gave him one, with a hoe, in them weeds. He stuck it for half an hour or thereabouts, then when Arnison came to see how they were getting on, he throwed the hoe at him and said, "Here, take the damn thing and do it yourself. I've fought the French, and I've fought the blackies, but I'm damned if I'll fight these 'ere weeds, they beat all." He put on his jacket, and a ragged 'un it were too, and off he went. Never asked for no money, no nothing, just went.' Then Father would add with a chuckle, 'He'd fought the French, and he'd fought the blackies, but they there thistles beat him!' So Joseph Briggs lived on because of his wagon; and the Duke's old soldier, because the thistles were particularly high one year.

Books were my only escape just then, they were there to hide in at every spare moment, nothing else was worth bothering about. There was no idea of educating myself or reading with any purpose in mind, books were just the drug that made life tolerable. Mother made no comment, she could guess pretty well the state I was in, but Father was puzzled and almost angry. 'You'll get no good sticking your head in them books every spare minute,' he said times enough. 'You've got your living to earn, mooning about won't help. Why don't you take an interest in something, save up and buy yourself a bike. Be like the other chaps, get out a bit. You'll never be any good at your work if you don't give your mind to it.' He could see no reason at all why I shouldn't give my mind to it. Everybody else did. But if there was one thing that I was certain of just then, it was that somehow, someday, I was going to get out of that sort of life. How that was going to be done it was impossible to say; there seemed no earthly chance of a break in the wall of isolation and ignorance that shut me in, but something had got to happen sometime, some opportunity, some plan would develop, till then it was just a case of hanging on.

Father got really worried. He was afraid that I might shut myself up in a fantasy life of my own, as his mother had done; then people would think I was cracked, and there was no telling what might happen. He put it all down to mooning about all the time, alone, and getting so wrapped up in books. If I were to mix up with the other chaps a bit I'd get like them in time, and then everything would be all right. So he put me down for the Ancient Shepherds, though by rights they ought not to take anybody under eighteen. The Shepherds were a benefit club that paid four shillings a week to any of their members who were ill and off work; but they met once a fortnight up at the Pheasant, and altogether there was a good deal going on round the Shepherds. Apart from Church and Chapel it was the liveliest thing in Byfield.

They had a room of their own that ran out over the stable at the Pheasant. Willie Potter let them have it rent-free because he supplied the beer, and it was the best custom he had. Generally there wasn't much doing at the Pheasant, there wasn't enough money about for that. On a Saturday night there might be as many as half a dozen men up there, with a pint apiece, which they were making last while they played a slow game of dominoes or had a go at the darts. At other times there was never anybody much. A few regulars used it. Bob Gregory called there with his van on market days, to see if there was anything for him to pick up, and always had a pint. The insurance man stopped there for half a pint to eat with his sandwiches when he was on his weekly round, and a drunken fishmonger, who called with herrings when he felt like it, was a bit more generous with his custom, but nobody else. If it had not been for the fortnightly meeting of the Ancient Shepherds, Willie would not have sold enough to keep the place open.

An old wooden ladder with a handrail to it led up from the yard at the back of the public house to the loft, where the meeting was held. I followed Father up, wondering what was going to happen, because the Ancient Shepherds were very secret about their meetings and did everything behind locked doors and with a great deal of mystery. There was a little cubby hole at the top which, when we went in and shut the door, was quite dark. Voices could be heard somewhere behind the partition. It was all a bit eerie. There was no way through the partition that I could see. Father gave a signal, three slow raps on the wall in front. A little panel, about three inches square, shot back and a severe-looking eye under a bushy eyebrow stared out at us. A voice, it sounded like Johnny Batson's, enquired sharply, 'Who is without?' Father's knowledge of the ritual must have given out at this point, because he just said, 'Me.' 'Give the password,' said Johnny. 'I forget it,' said Father. The panel clicked shut, and we could hear Johnny call out, 'Brother Hillyer seeks to enter without the password.' A pause, as if the person spoken to was occupied at the moment, and then a voice answered crisply, 'Admit him.' A door in the partition opened, not too quickly, and Johnny let us in, grumbling, 'You've forgot the password again, Bob.' Johnny took his duties as portal keeper seriously, and to be robbed of the password was annoying. 'Well, I be in all right, ain't I?' said Father cheerfully. 'Yes, you be in all right,' said Johnny, with a sarcasm that plainly meant, 'if you call appearing in this clumsy, improper sort of way getting in.' We were in the secret place of the Shepherds! There was a patch of light to one side of the room, but all the rest was in shadow. It was just possible to make out, through the gloom and the thick haze of shag, about a dozen men sitting on a bench with beer mugs beside them. Away in a corner were three or four young chaps, also with beer mugs and tobacco, but obviously not used to it, and a bit overawed.

Resplendent under the hanging lamp that made the patch of light sat Billy Makins, the president, behind a table, with his collar of office on, and Willie Potter, the secretary, beside him, with a large account book and a tin cash-box for the money, all ready. It was about the only secretarial job in the village that Mr Wickens did not do, but as schoolmaster he considered himself to be above this sort of thing, to belong to the gentry in fact, and to be superior to such a merely working-class affair as the Ancient Shepherds. Johnny Batson, with a long white wand in his hand, stood beside the official table, ready to execute all lawful commands as fast as his sore feet would let him. It all looked dark and desperate, like a cave full of robbers. The yellow gleam of the big oil lamp was all the light there was and Billy Makins got all the benefit of that. But you couldn't imagine him as a very ferocious kind of robber chief, he was fat and cheerful, and he had a right to be, with a nice little jobbing builder's business like his. The broad blue presidential collar, with the brass sheep dangling from it, as if somebody was going to sling it up somewhere, was a very imposing thing on a man as well filled out as Billy. Willie Potter, as the secretary, had a smaller collar with a pen on the end.

If the Shepherds ever went in for excitement there was not much about that night. The men with the beer mugs exchanged a word or two now and then; those of us who were waiting to join wondered what was coming and kept quiet. A few more men came in, and Willie nodded to each of them and said, 'Pint as usual?' When he had got enough orders he called downstairs, and his wife came in with the pints on a tray. The president drank whisky, to show that he could afford it. The secret life of the Ancient Shepherds was not very thrilling. Nobody seemed to be in much of a hurry. The beer was all drunk at last, and there were no more orders. Willie

Potter shut up his book, locked the tin cash-box, and said something to the president. Billy Makins straightened himself, arranged his collar, and put on a big pair of blue cuffs which he had taken off earlier on because they got in the way of his whisky, and began to look important and ready for business. Johnny Batson brightened up; with feet like his, standing about was painful, as well as boring, but Johnny liked a bit of ceremony and the prospect of it made up for a lot. 'You boys come over here now,' he called, 'and stop that grinning,' he added severely. 'Wipe that silly look off your faces. This ain't no comic show. Behave yourselves.' We did our best to oblige, but it was hard not to feel foolish, and it was harder still when Billy Makins put on a three-cornered hat, like a mayor wears, and Johnny brought out a great, gold-painted shepherd's crook for him to hold, and Billy said in a deep, solemn voice, 'Let the portal be barred.' He enjoyed this dressing-up, and made the most of it, though the natural comic in him showed through a bit. Johnny went over and shook the door, for the form's sake, though it had been locked all the evening. He stumped back and lined us up in front of the president. Willie Potter read something out of a book that was full of long, important-sounding words which had Willie bothered a good deal. Then each of us in turn was given the crook to hold, and swore 'on this sacred symbol of the shepherd's ancient craft' to be true and faithful shepherds, and never to divulge what went on at the meetings. There wasn't anything to divulge that I could see; still, when Billy gave us what he called 'the right hand of fellowship' we stopped feeling silly and felt important.

But there was more to the Ancient Shepherds than just the meetings. There was the annual dinner, for instance, in the first week of the new year, that was something! Mr Du Cane, when he bothered to come, sat on Billy's right hand, and the Rector on his left, because they each subscribed five guineas to the club. The eating and drinking was practically unlimited. Billy Makins sang his funniest songs, and they kept it up as late as ten o'clock, sometimes. Then there was the procession to church on the first Sunday in October. Johnny led it with his wand, then came the two oldest members with the club banner, then the rest of the club, with the president and the secretary in the rear, though without their regalia which were secret to the meetings. Sometimes there was even a band, if anybody knew of one that would come cheap, for the practice. Before we started Willie Potter gave everybody in the procession a blue rosette, as big as a tea plate with a red ribbon all across it, on which was written in silver paint the words 'The Most Noble Order of Ancient Shepherds'. He took them out of a biscuit tin and put them back in it again when we had finished. The Rector preached a special sermon about self-help, and said what an encouraging thing it was to see such a fine body of men, united in the cause of assisting the unfortunate. There was something in that, of course, because if a man was ill and did not belong to the Shepherds, he was in for a bad time, because his pay would be stopped at work. But it wasn't only that. There was the glory of walking in the procession, and the fill-out at the dinner. And it gave a man a chance to have a pint now and then without his wife kicking up about his going to a public house. He had got to go up there to pay his dues, anyway. There was a lot to be got out of the Shepherds, but not for me. I was odd man all the time. So I stopped going, what was the use? The dinner and the procession were all right, so I turned up at them, but I gave the meetings a miss and got Father to pay my dues.

So the days drifted along, with now and then those casual moments of insight that came when they would, and left a freshened interest in life behind them. But when it died away, there was the old heavy slog again, with nothing particular to look forward to, nothing ahead, just going round and round like a man in gaol, desperately considering ways of getting out, and with about as much chance of doing so. Most people who wanted to get away from Byfield went off to a relative somewhere, and got work there, but we hadn't got any relatives, except those in London, and there was no chance with them. Still, depressed and often miserable as I was, the obstinate resolve never left me that somehow, sometime, I would break out of the circumstances that hemmed me in. I would have a life of my own, and some self-respect. That I wanted above everything, something to bolster up my pride in myself, something that I could do, and which the silly lot who thought me just a freak and a fool couldn't do; something, no matter what, that would bring reassurance.

By now I had gone over everything in Stubbs's shop, but every few weeks he would hear of a sale somewhere and go off to see what he could pick up cheap. He generally came back with a cartload of broken-down furniture and assorted junk that kept him busy for a while, and as often as not there were books among it. One Saturday night he left me to turn over a tin bath full of empty bottles, chipped mantel ornaments, odd slippers, boot-trees, doorknobs, and things like that. As I tipped them out, a grimy bundle of books tied up with string fell out with them. There was one thick one, and half a dozen slim ones, all covered with dust, as if they had been tied up like that for years. The string was rotten and broke as I picked them up, so that the bundle disintegrated all over the floor. They were old school books, and in Latin. There was a dictionary, some that looked to be poetry, and several others. They had been used a good deal at one time, for they were heavily thumbed and scrawled all over with English words and phrases, as if whoever had owned them had needed all the help he could get. I flicked over the pages; there was no name anywhere, but scribbled all over the title page of the dictionary, in faded ink, was the bold statement, 'If anybody takes this book I will punch his nose in the bogs after tea.' It could have been a caution, but it was more likely a defiance, a kind of general challenge to anybody who fancied himself to try it out in the bogs, after tea, with the dictionary as the gauge of battle. I warmed to the boy who wrote that. He wasn't a bully, that was certain, a bully wouldn't risk all comers like that. Half the endpapers and title pages had disappeared; there was nothing to tell who he was, or his school, but he seemed like a friend. I flicked through the books again. They were in Latin. I could learn Latin from them! There was the grammar, which had given its former owner a lot of trouble by the look of it, because it was dirtier, more dog-eared, more loose-leafed and scrawled over than any of the other books, but it all seemed to be there. It was called *Arnold Henry's First*

Latin Book. Arnold reminded me of Dr Arnold, in *Tom Brown's School Days*, but it couldn't be anything to do with him. Latin could be learned from it though. Scholars knew Latin, real scholars like Dr Brearley who used to come to the rectory. To know Latin would be something, and here in my hands was the means of gaining it.

I got 'mensa' by heart that very night, and felt two feet taller when I had finished. I had mastered the first declension! Some of the rich fruits of the Latin grammar were already mine! Nobody else in Byfield knew as much Latin as I did, except the Rector. Mr Wickens had never learned any, I was sure. This was a distinction to hug to myself, and keep my self-respect warm with. Sustained by it I plodded on, learning page after page of the tattered little book. Among the rubbish in the furniture stall was an old abridgement of somebody's *Roman History*. Turning it over times enough before, it had seemed too dry to bother with, but now it was just the thing for the background of what I had to learn. Soon it was possible to make some sort of sense of the exercises in the grammar, and then to pick about in the other books. They were selections from Caesar and some Virgil. My friend, the puncher of noses, had written a good deal of the translation between the lines, and, providing no doubt against anticipated trouble, had made notes on difficult bits of the grammar. It was all very helpful of him. With something definite to do the time did not drag by so heavily.

Chapter 15

When I could keep clear of Spicer's evil rages things were not too bad. Morning and evening there was the milking to be done, and cows are animals that are easy to get along with. There is always something confidential about a cow, you can trust her. Most of the rest of the day was spent tagging about the fields, fetching and carrying for Johnson. In a sort of way I got to like him, and I think he felt the same about me; though he yelled and cursed at times, there was no malice in it, give him five minutes and it was over. But when I had to drive plough for Spicer life was foul: it would have been pleasanter to be with the devil, for they say he is a very civilised person, but Spicer was a beast. Winter and summer the working day was long.

It is a quarter past five in the morning; getting out of bed into the cold, damp air of the bedroom, lighting the candle with shirt tails flapping round bare legs, and huddling on cold clothes is depressing. If John is away, and there is nobody to talk to, the business of getting dressed at that time in the morning is grimmer still. I creep downstairs, as quietly as I can, so as not to wake Mother, who is a light sleeper and never gets really off till near morning. It is pitch dark on the stairs but I know every twist and knot in their warped old steps. Downstairs, there is just the light of the newly started fire tumbling about the room as the flames from the dry sticks rise and fall in the chimney place. Father has got his pipe started and is leaning forward, with the teapot in his hand, watching for the kettle to boil; and smoking very contentedly, his weather-beaten face full of quiet pleasure in the enjoyment of the moment. While I crush my protesting feet into heavy boots, board-hard from standing near the fireplace to dry all night, he makes the tea and pours me out a large cupful. He swallows his own down quickly, and puts the cosy over the teapot to keep it warm until Mother comes down, gives his pipe one or two quick puffs to brighten it up a bit and then goes out, quickly, as he has above a mile to walk to his work. I am in no particular hurry. Johnson's farm is only about five minutes away. It is nice to be alone for a while, with the fire to look at, and a cup full of hot tea between my hands. There has been rain in the night, and the last leaves that still cling to the bushes hang wet and dejected. It is just growing light enough to see that they are there, the stars seem withdrawing further and further away. The tea is warm inside, I am settled into my clothes, there is something quiet and all my own about the morning. In front of me the path, without footsteps to mark it since the rain fell, looks bright and new; even the muddy places have been flattened out and catch what light there is on their wet surfaces. For the five minutes that it takes to walk to work I am alone, in a friendly world.

But it does not last long. The cowshed door is already open; I can see that as I take a short cut into the farmyard, over the wall and between the dark shapes of the ricks; and the dim light of old Eli's lantern is bobbing about as he gets ready for milking. Eli will have been there a good twenty minutes already, and walked the better part of two miles from his house before that. He is getting on for seventy, a little man, spare of body, with a brown, shrivelled face, and entirely bald. Now he hangs his lantern up and starts tying on the filthy piece of sacking which he uses for an apron. Perhaps he will grunt 'Hullo' as I come in. Perhaps he won't; it depends on the mood he is in. I slip past him, and either he does not notice that I am there or does not feel like talking, for he says nothing. I have the candle lit in my lantern, have my own equally filthy apron on, and have sat down with the bucket between my knees, beside my first cow, by the time the church clock strikes six. If I were a minute late in getting down to work Eli would start growling at me for being behind time, and being too lazy to get up in a morning, and wonder what my dad thought he was up to, in letting me hang about of a morning like that. But I don't mind Eli, that sort of thing is just his routine. He is a quiet old man as a rule, and easy enough to get on with if you fall into his ways. He goes through the day like a machine, not talking much, or thinking much about what he is doing, it is all habit by now; but if he falls a few minutes behind his schedule he gets upset. 'Every pesky thing is bothersome today,' he would fret, 'I be all behind, I be all behind.' He never uses stronger language for he is a good chapel man. I can hear him quieting a restive cow as I settle down to my own. 'Quiet now. Keep that pesky tail to yourself. Stand still I say. Stand still.' Eli's voice blends with all the other sounds, sights and smells, and is part of the early morning. The lantern beside me throws interesting shadows, but I am too cosy to notice them much as I snuggle up to the warm flank of the cow, whose steadily working jaws take in a continuous stream of hay; and there is the rhythmical swish of the milk that streams, warm and white, from her teats, and the rich, sweet smell that rises from it. Everything is very pleasant and drowsy. It is an effort to get up and go from one cow to another. When I have done seven I have finished my lot.

Now I have really to wake up and the day is properly beginning. My first real job of a morning is to take a pail of milk across to the farmhouse, so that they can have fresh milk for breakfast. When I have handed that over to Johnson's housekeeper, I must go to the wood pile and bring in a dry faggot for the back kitchen fire. It will be sunrise in a little while: to the eastward the early morning sky shows streaks of colour, as if somebody has scrabbled red and yellow paint along it. All there is to do with the fire is to lay the faggot across the iron dogs in the huge old fireplace, stuff a newspaper under it, light it and away she goes; the flames crackling and leaping up the wide chimney, bursting into a roar as all the wood catches hold, and the sparks flash and fall, and the dark little room becomes alive with swiftly moving light. Two great pots hang on sooty chains from a bar across the chimney, and these supply all the boiling water that the farm needs for scalding milk buckets, mixing calves' food, and things like that. As soon as the faggot is well alight I get a few minutes to myself, and Miss Kirby, the housekeeper, brings me my breakfast, bread and something to put on it, butter sometimes, but more often dripping or goosefat, and they are as good as butter any day. The bread is generally ends of loaves, but crisp and tasty. It is nice sitting there, gulping hot tea, watching the fire and eating. If I want to I can learn a bit of

Latin grammar too, if I have got any copied out on paper in my pocket, but I haven't always got any and I don't always want to; and in any case I am careful not to let anybody see me at it. Before I have finished Miss Kirby is sure to come fussing out. She is an old worrier, always flustered about something, but she has come down in the world; once she lived with a brother who had a farm of his own, but now she has to earn a living for herself, and is frightened that she may not please. 'You must hurry up, Richard. The master has nearly finished his breakfast. He was clearing up his bacon when I came out. You know what he will say if you are not ready when he is. Hurry up now!'

I know what he will say; I have heard it all before. If, in five minutes or so, I am not waiting for him, with two fair-sized bags of corn slung over my shoulder, I shall be in for it. Every day, when he is at home, he goes out to look at his sheep, first thing after breakfast. Sheep are silly things and need looking over every day, or else they are in trouble. Johnson liked to do it himself. If he was in a good mood he would come out whistling, crush his billycock on to his head, pick up his paddle from the porch, and set out in style. I just fall in behind with the bags of corn, neither of us speaking. All I see of him is the back of his tweed coat and bedford cord breeches. The paddle was a light pole, like a broomstick, with a small blade at one end; he used it to root up thistles or any particularly obnoxious-looking weed that he saw on the way; and it came in handy to drive animals with, or to point at things that he wanted done. On good mornings it was also a staff of dignity. With every step, he planted it down in front of him, just a little to one side of his line of advance, and then, with an unbending arm, swung it round on the pivot of its blade in as wide an arc as he could compass, walking as erect as a drum major glorying with his baton. On mornings of this sort, he would throw an occasional word over his shoulder for my benefit, as I struggled along behind him with the corn. It was never anything very much, a question sometimes, or an order, or perhaps a comment; made as much to himself as to me, about something which caught his eye in the fields, never anything you could call conversation. One morning, surprisingly, he asked, 'You read Shakespeare at that school? Mr Wickens teach you Shakespeare, eh?' 'Yes sir, we read *The Tempest* once.' 'You did, did you; I bet you don't know any of it.' 'I do, some.' 'Well, say it then.' And plodding along over the soggy fields with my load, I repeated the piece about 'The cloud-capped towers, the gorgeous palaces', and for the moment forgot that my hands were almost frozen in the raw air, that the corn felt as heavy as a bag full of shot, and that at any moment it might slip from my numbed fingers, and knowing the charmed words, I was, for a second or two, the equal of my master. He heard me out, but all he said was, 'Well, so you do!'

On bad mornings he would come out scowling, with his flustered housekeeper hovering around holding his hat or something he wanted, and he would call me several different kinds of fool for putting too much corn, or too little, into the bags; and instead of stalking along in a lordly way with the paddle, he would hold it by the extreme end of the handle and jab the blade at things, and big trouble was only a matter of waiting until we got to the first bunch of sheep. We always began with the lot that was furthest away. As soon as they saw us coming they would start trotting up and gather round, jostling and shoving, to get a few grains of corn each; it was only meant as bait, to bring them up for inspection, and looking solemn, and silly, and smelling of grease. The ritual then was that I held the bag on my knee, so as not to dirty it by putting it down on the wet ground, untied the string, and waited for him to take out the few handfuls he wanted there; tied it up again, and put the bag somewhere safe, and waited. Johnson would stand and brood a while, watching the sheep snuffling round. Suddenly he would point and call, 'That one!' I make a dash at the animal he wants. Sometimes I am lucky and get it and manage to hold on, more often than not it gets away, or some tough old wether, with a kick like a mule, knocks me on to the ground and is all over me; and Johnson dances about in a rage and catches the beast himself, and swears, and wonders what he pays me five shillings a week for when I am not worth sixpence. It was a silly business, funny too, I expect, for anybody who was not mixed up in it; but it was no fun for me, rolling on the wet ground with the dirty hooves of a sheep trampling all over my face. Johnson would curse and wave his paddle about, but no matter how many times in a morning we went through that performance, he generally simmered down before we got back home; and even when he was in a flaming temper he was always gentle with the animals. He was a queer man in many ways, he hadn't any friends or any relations that anybody knew about; he didn't belong to our countryside. On market days he got half seas over, but never what you could call drunk; all his life lay in his farm, the animals, and the things that grew on it. There must have been something in him that Byfield never got to know about: he was a hard man, but neither cruel nor sensual.

That autumn there was a lot of horse-buying. The war had just started, and the army, starved for transport, would take practically anything that was on four legs. There was money to be made out of horses, and Johnson was after it. He was all over the place in his yellow-wheeled gig, with our John. Sometimes they would be away for a night, and next day John would come riding in with a string of horses, sitting bare-back on the first one and having no more trouble with the other five or six than if they were pet lambs. John was a wonder with animals. I wished I could be, because with him away so much I had to drive plough, and for me that was a hideous job. Spicer was the horse-keeper, a surly beast at the best of times, but my performances drove him into prancing fury. In a general way a good farm horse knew its work by heart, and could carry on with next to no help from a driver; but with the war, and the scarcity, Johnson let all his best go, and we were left with the screws, the wall-eyed, the lame and the untamable beasts which smart sellers had slipped into the string at one time or another, and even the most hard-pressed army vet could not bring himself to accept.

They might begin all right, if they were in the mood. I would put the foremost into the furrow and start them off, smacking the whip and hoping that for this time at any rate they would be taken in by it. For a turn or two everything would be all right. There was the slap and rattle of the harness, the smell of horse sweat as the animals warmed to their work, the tearing sound of the stubbled earth as the ploughshare wrenched it from its place and sent it flowing steadily back along the breadboard to lie in a yellow ribbon, wet and shining in the chilly sun. Slowly my heart would steady down. It was going to be all right. Today I would get away with it. Then something would happen, anything. The sudden scream of a stone, perhaps, as it shrieked against the steel; or a bird, rising with a quick whirr of wings from under the horses' feet; and one of them would jump aside and trample the ploughed earth, and the others, feeling the pull change, would turn round to see what was going on, and get mixed up, and frightened, and there would be chaos beyond my power to straighten. Spicer hangs on to the plough handles as long as he can, cursing and yelling at me what to do, and turning the conflicting fears inside me into pulverised fright; then lets go, dashes at the horse, curses it, beats it, kicks it, his heavy boot coming up with savage impact on the smooth, tight skin of the horse's belly, wrenching, twisting, mauling the team back into the furrow.

Somehow they get started again, and I keep out of his way while he throws clods at me, which I dodge, and threatens what he will do when we get to the other side of the field and he can let go of the plough. To the misery of my own frightened futility is added all the misery of that brutal attack on the silly animals, that I could have saved from such treatment if I had only known how to handle them. The pain the poor beasts had to undergo tore at the heart, and the savage frenzy of the man as he beat and bludgeoned them seemed to come out of hell. Foul-mouthed and angry with me as he was, you could see he liked that beastliness; he enjoyed the impact of his boot on the quivering flesh, the sharp jab of pain that made the horse jump and shudder in its chains. He was loathsome, hateful: before even such animals as these it was a compliment to call him a beast. If he had just raved and threatened, it wouldn't have mattered so much; I wouldn't have cared if he had taken a swipe at me now and then, because I could have kept out of his way, but his convulsive fury seemed to be the man himself, naked in evil, and his foul language the boiling over of the filth that filled him. A consuming loathing and dread of him took possession of me. There was hardly any rest from it, because at night, when I went to bed, I knew that there was only an hour or two and it would all start again, and the thought of the next day was as hideous as the day itself. Even now, dregs of that fear wash about at the back of my mind, to break through occasionally and stain better things.

Nobody knew what was going on. Johnson was busy with his horse-buying and never came near, and I said nothing at home. What was the use? Barky Britnell was cutting a hedge at the bottom of the field, where we were ploughing, and every time our circus came by he would stare at us over his shoulder, wild-eyed and curious; like a ragged gnome, half hidden by the bushes he was chopping and pulling into place; but Barky wasn't anybody. We got up level to where he was working. There had been the usual amount of trouble that morning, and Spicer was working up towards his foulest mood. The leader was a gaunt old horse with a great lump on his near hind leg; but he could still do a steady day's work in a team, and had more sense than most, so he was kept at it. He plodded on down the furrow, until he caught sight of Barky, just in front of him, and bushes moving; he had never seen them directly in his line of vision before. It struck him as odd. He stopped to think it over. I shouted at him, and then gave him a flick with the whip, but he wouldn't move. Spicer glowered and cursed. I went to the old horse's head and tried to pull him on; but he backed away, and crowded the horses behind him on to the plough and over the newly turned earth. Beside himself with rage, Spicer dashed at the team, his plough paddle beating furiously down on the poor old beast's head; who backed frantically away, until he got his leg over the plough chains, and the whole mixed-up bunch milled around, and kicked and snapped at each other. Mad with passion Spicer lifted his great boot and kicked at the lump on the old horse's leg, until the iron-shod toe was ploughing through the spurting blood and pus of the broken tumour, and the poor beast screamed with agony. Everything was blotted out in me but the horse's cries, the blood and the foul image of Spicer. I flung myself on him, punching at him in a blind frenzy, beating at him with the whip handle, yelling again and again, 'Let the horse alone, you filthy great beast.' He threw me off, then came at me, whirling the paddle, ready for murder in the violence of this last outbreak. Backing from him I tripped and fell on the rough ground, and he was over me with his weapon; while for one infinite second life throbbed in me, and waited for the heavy blade to smash down and end it. There was a scuffle. Barky had burst out of the hedge, torn the paddle from Spicer and, with a great, swinging blow of it, almost broken his arm before flinging it away and darting back to the safety of the hedge again;

where he crouched among the bushes, vicious, alert, furious as a cornered stoat. Spicer knew better than to go after him. He stood holding his arm and swearing, 'You mad old devil, if you hadn't got that axe I'd cut your damned guts out.' For a minute or two he raged and threatened while I watched him warily; but he was not going to try anything, so I went back to the horses. Left to themselves they had quieted down, and it was not a hard job to straighten them out. The rage and fear in me died away, coming back in uncontrollable bursts at the sight of the old horse's torn and bleeding sore. Cruelty like that was hideous, hateful, never had I seen anything like it. Animals might be neglected a bit or overworked; they were part of our life, you took them for granted, they had to put up with things as we did, but deliberately to make them suffer was hellish. Barky had saved me from bad trouble, perhaps saved my life. Why did he burst out like that? Perhaps, in his mixed-up mind, Mother and I were one, and with her he was like a dog with its mistress.

That time when we were ploughing stretched on endlessly. I expect that it took about three weeks really, but it seemed years. Only once was there anything like a pleasant break in the miserable days. Hunting had begun, and the hounds were about the fields. We saw them first topping a rise in the distance, and Spicer was away like a shot after gate money. The team stood still, they were always ready to do that, I'll say that for them, and I watch. There are red and black dots racing across the wintry meadows in our direction. The cattle grazing there stand for a minute or two, alert and uneasy, and then move out of the way before the pack gets too near. I can see the hounds now, strung out, with their noses to the ground, eager in their running. The whole hunt is making directly towards us. There is a quick glimpse of the fox himself as he slips through the hedge on to the grass verge of the plough land. He looks as if he has come a good way, but he still has his wits about him and starts along a furrow which will keep him out of sight a bit, and bring the pack on to the freshly turned earth where the going will be hard enough to slow them up a little; and give him more chance of getting into the long drain at the other end of the field, which is plainly what he is making for. Spicer has spotted which way the hunt is running, and tears off to the gate which leads into the plough land. Barky has seen it too, and gets there first. There is a fight for a minute; but Spicer's great flailing arms overwhelm the little man. He is down in the mud, then up again. Spicer is kicking at him now and he slinks off along the hedgerow, and Spicer has the gate. He is in for a good thing with that gate.

The hounds are through the hedge and on to the sticky going, over the freshly ploughed land. Tom Fallows, the huntsman, is close up and is first through the gate; for the hedge just there has not been cut yet and is a stiff affair, and Tom has too much sense to risk his neck when he needn't. Close after Tom come the red coats. They are checked a little at the gate, partly because the mud is deep there and the dressy ones don't want to ruin their white cords if they can help it. A few hot-headed ones dash through and on to the grass verge, spattered from head to foot; their proud horses, with reins lathering their necks, scattering the slush in all directions. Spicer stands holding the gate open, with his cap in his hand. 'Good luck to your Lordship. Here's my cap. Good luck to your Lordship. Thank you, your Lordship.' Everybody with a red coat is a lord to a gate opener in the hunting field. The black coats come pushing and shoving through in a gang. 'Good luck to you, Sir John. Good luck to you, sir. Here's my cap. Good luck to you, sir. Good luck and thank you.' The press is through the gate now and on to the headland, avoiding the ploughed land as much as they can. The fox has reached the mouth of the drain and the hounds are milling round it, balked and angry. The first horsemen have come up and reined in to see what Tom Fallows will do. Spicer is beginning to shut the gate. He is going over to the drain, to see what he can pick up there, no doubt. He has done well by the look of it; his cap hangs heavy as he scoops out the contents and puts them into his pocket. That is always a good gate, nobody will face that old black-thorn hedge if they can help it. But there is a late one coming up. He has been off, by the look of him, for there is clay all down one side where he hit the ground. There is no sense in holding a gate open for chaps like him. He will just gallop through, making out that he is in too much of a hurry to put his hand into his pocket and give you something. That is what I thought. Spicer has let the gate swing to, and has started to walk away. The late comer has pulled up, and shouts to him to come back and open it. So he comes back, and there is his cap stuck out again. 'Good luck to you, sir. Good luck to you,' and something falls into the cap, sixpence by the way Spicer takes it out. He is lucky! With that sort it might only be a penny. He has done well today, and is certain to be up at the Pheasant tonight, throwing his weight about.

Over by the drain they look pretty baffled. That fox knew what he was up to when he got in there; because pipes run out in all directions, and he might be in any one of them. It is no use trying to dig him out, and if a terrier went in after him the dog might lose himself, or get stuck, and be more trouble than enough. Of course, by rights there should be a grating at the mouth of the drain to stop just this very thing happening, but it was pulled up only a week or two ago when there was a bit of a flood and it was easier to pull the grating out and let the water off that way than clean it. Somebody will get into trouble for that. The hounds draw off. Tom Fallows leads them away, making for the cover down Holly Road, to see if they can find another fox. A good part of the hunt follows them, the rest go home, they have had enough.

Spicer comes back pleased with himself. He must have had a good day. He is almost joking! 'So you managed to keep that fine lot of horses still while I was away. Wonderful! Wonderful!' His good humour, if you can call it that, has to be shown off on Barky. 'Hi, you silly old devil,' he gloats, 'I got thirty bob at that gate. Thought you were going to get it, didn't you? Not you! I'll break your damned neck if you get in my way again.' For weeks after, whenever he saw him, he would say, 'Had any hunting money lately, Barky?' It was his idea of a joke. For the rest of the day we had no trouble, perhaps because his better temper got into the horses, perhaps because he was quieter and didn't bluster and swear so much about everything, perhaps because it just happened that way; but the team settled to its work and we finished in moderate peace.

Chapter 16

That was the first winter of the Kaiser's war. There was a great buzz of excitement about it everywhere. Eli, who was a long-headed man and read the papers, said, 'You mark my words, this war will do the working man a lot of good. I shouldn't be surprised if farm men's wages aren't up to as much as a pound a week before it's over.' The rest of the men thought that sounded a bit wild; still, they might go up a shilling or two and that would be worth having. Nobody thought much about soldiers getting killed, it was the dash and glory of the thing that occupied them just then. They talked about the Boer War and thought that this would be much the same sort of affair, only it would be over a lot quicker, and be on a grander scale, and nearer home. We should be fighting the German army rather than a lot of farmers; so it would be a more professional kind of set-to altogether. But it would not last long. There would be certain to be a smashing great battle somewhere or other, rather like Waterloo, which we would win of course, and it would all be over by Christmas.

The Yeomanry were called up. Crowds of people went to see them get their horses and accoutrements in the cattle market at Billington. It was a sight to remember, all those hundreds of saddles slung over the iron rail they used for tying bullocks up to; and it was as good as a show, watching the fellows, some of them clerks and people like that, who didn't know much about horses, getting thrown off, and losing their mounts and trying to catch them again. Still, nobody thought that the Yeomanry would have much to do with the war. Men who were too old to go, and young ones who hadn't enlisted, envied them what would probably be not much more than a ride through Germany. We had no idea that the world was coming to an end.

Father got very worked up about the war. It came as a great crimson splash of excitement into his drab life. The starved romantic in him delighted in all the heroics, the bustle and the noise. It was something to talk about, and argue over. We were going to beat the Germans, and that made everybody feel big. Old soldiers, who had fought in Africa or Egypt, were listened to with respect, their opinions sought and quoted. Splendid illustrated magazines started coming out; with magnificent pictures, all drawn by 'Our Own Artist at the Front', of cavalry charges, and gallant young officers waving their swords and leading their men against the vicious-looking but obviously beaten enemy; with shells exploding all around them, like fireworks; and if there were no dead bodies about, because they might depress the readers, some of the men had bloody bandages round their heads, to show how desperate was the fighting. Father took in one of these, though it cost him threepence a week, a quarter of his pocket money; and spent the winter evenings spelling out the war stories, though reading was not his strong point, and it didn't come easily. That Christmas, instead of the meat tea, the Rector gave every house a pound of tea, done up in a wonderful tin that had a picture on the front of General French and General Joffre shaking hands, a sailor and a soldier, one on each side, and Admiral Jellicoe on the lid. When people got that they took the tea out at once and put the tin up on the mantelpiece, where they could see it all the time.

At first, when the Yeomanry had gone, the war seemed a long way from us, but it got nearer, and more real, as the months went by. There was talk that Lord Postern had given Hetton Down to the War Office as a place for a camp. It was a bare patch of chalky hillside, about three miles away, no good for anything except to graze a few sheep. Then people who went up that way said that the camp was already started, and there were soldiers there. Going up to look at them became a regular Sunday afternoon trip. Mother said that she would like to go, so we hired Bob Gregory's wagonette; and then, at the last minute, she changed her mind and said we should all have our bellyfull of soldiers and soldiering before the war was over, and she didn't want to go. So Father and John and I went in state in the wagonette. Bob Gregory came with us, because he would never let anybody else but himself drive his old horse; people said that it was because if anybody pushed him out of his regular shambling trot he would drop down dead. There was quite a little procession of people going up to the Down that afternoon, though it wasn't much of a day for weather. From the road, at the top of the ridge, we would be able to look down on the camp, if there was one.

It was there all right. Already the turf was cut up in all directions by vehicles and men and animals coming and going. The troops were living in tents, pitched in the middle of this mess in the best Boer War fashion, in the form of a hollow square, with a chewed-up parade ground in the middle, and a tall fir tree, roughly barked, for a flagstaff. We pulled up at the side of the road, among all the other carts and traps and wagonettes. There was a church service just beginning. The men were drawn up on the parade ground, getting the full force of the sharp gusts of wind and squally rain that scoured along the bleak hillside. Some of them were in uniform, and they were in a squad by themselves, the rest were in civilian clothes, just as they had left home. Some had smart suits and bowler hats on; others, who had more sense, or who didn't care so much about impressing the recruiting officer, had come in rough working clothes, with heavy boots and cloth caps. They were not much to look at, but you could see that they felt themselves to be in the army; and they had already got a band together, which was drawn up in a ring in front of the flagstaff. The parson had a little wooden stand, just alongside. He began to preach. We couldn't catch what he was saying, but you could see that he was struggling to make all the men hear by the way he swayed his body backwards and forwards. Then he closed his book. The men turned over some leaflets that they had in their hands and the band started to play a hymn tune, one that I knew very well, because we had it often in church, a deep, solemn thing that suited a brass band and men's voices. 'Holy, holy, holy, Lord God Almighty, All thy works shall praise thy name in earth, and sky, and sea.' But the tune had never sounded like this before. It filled my heart and began to push tears out of my eyes. It sharpened all consciousness, that of standing up in a wagonette that was pulled into the gutter of an ill-made, dirty road; of the old horse, drooping in the shafts, and of the smell of him that was in the rugs, and the cushions, and the vehicle itself; and yet feeling all that with the outside of me, the innermost, living part being out there with the men and the music. The band stopped, leaving an emptiness and an ache. The men marched round for a minute, and then broke up and went off to their draggled tents on the waterlogged turf.

As we pottered along home, Bob Gregory said that if that was soldiering it had changed since his day. Father said that they would be 'all right when the frost came, and hardened the ground up a bit'. Only the frost did not come. The raw, wet weather went on week after week, nobody remembered anything like it happening before; it was as strange in its way as the war itself. The chalky hillside churned up under the men's feet into a grey, gluey mud that worked its way into everything, and plastered itself over everything, and refused to be cleaned off; even if they had anything to clean it off with, which they hadn't. Many of the men were miners from the North, used to working underground in the warm; and here they were, living all the time in conditions which would have made the most weather-hardened labourers suffer. They caught pneumonia, and died by dozens. Billington hospital was full of them, so they took over a church hall, and soon that was full too; and still those who could walk about were left, shivering, on the bare hillside. At last somebody with a little sense came down from the War Office and ordered all the troops into billets until the spring, when the camp could be made fit to live in.

Some of the men were sent to Byfield, and we had one. He

stood outside our door one night, just as it was getting dark; a thin-faced little man in muddy khaki, with a paper in his hand which said we were to give him a billet. It was lucky that he had the paper, because we couldn't make much of what he said, his northern speech sounded like a foreign language. We hadn't a bed to spare, but Mother made one up for John and me in the barn, and gave him ours. She did her best to make him welcome, fried him some bacon and eggs and gave him an armchair by the fire; but though he tried to eat, he couldn't manage anything much, and just sat there, huddled up near the blaze, struggling to answer when we spoke to him; though you could see that it was an effort. 'It's my belief that chap is bad,' Mother said when he crept up to bed. 'He wants a doctor. You go up and tell that sergeant at the school I said so.' The sergeant looked comfortable enough. He had got the big stove glowing red-hot and was sitting on a box, with a bottle of beer on the floor beside him, eating something out of a tin. 'Tell your mam not to worry, lad,' he said, when I gave him the message. 'All he wants is a night's rest in the warm and dry. He will be right canny in the morning.' And the sergeant went on scooping his supper out of the tin.

But whatever canny meant, if it was anything good, our lodger wasn't it. He didn't turn up at breakfast time. Mother went and knocked on his door. No answer! She went in, but was out again immediately, looking upset. 'Richard, you go and fetch that sergeant. Tell him I want him at once, it's important.' He came, looked in the room for a minute, and then went away, and came back with two men and a stretcher, who carried something away on it that lay still under a blanket. We never knew what our sad little soldier was called, except that his first name was Arthur. 'They call me Arthur,' he had said, when he came in that evening. No more men turned up to sleep in our room so John and I got it back again, but not until Mother had scrubbed it out, and boiled the sheets, and had the window open for a couple of days. 'The room stinks of death,' she said. So did a lot of the soldiers that winter. There must have been many people up north that wondered what had gone wrong when the men whom they had cheered, and waved away to fight the Germans, got no further than a muddy death on a bleak hillside in the south of England. It was a strange feeling, getting back into the familiar bed: that was different now, because a man had just died in it, but John was in it too, solid and ordinary as usual, and that helped.

Somehow or other the dash and the colour went out of the war for me after that. Father still took in his magazine, and read it, and picked out the stories about the fighting in the Sunday paper; but even for him, I do not think that it was the same. That the war meant battles, and shells exploding, and famous generals, and daring men creeping out of the trenches at night to raid in no man's land was clear, because there it was in print; but it meant also living in sodden tents, and dying of bad weather, because we had seen that for ourselves. And running through all the war for me, the core and soul of it, was that group of men drawn up in the wind and the rain, so conscientiously being soldiers, while the deep music spoke of solemnities within and above them.

Most of the officers were quartered in Billington, and

between them they got up a theatrical show to pass the time away. They were supposed to have some real actors among them, and people who had never been to a theatre in their lives were anxious to go and see what it was like; and those who had been once, when they were on a visit to London, or something like that, looked forward to it as a bit of life, so there was a rush for the tickets. All I knew about shows was the concerts we had in the school sometimes; and I wanted to see this very badly, because actors and theatres were part of the life that educated people lived, and offered a delight that must be something special. Not that the old Assembly Rooms were much of a theatre, come to that, but the actors would make up for it. Nothing much happened there as a rule, except perhaps a dog show, or a political meeting, once in a while. The bills stuck up for these affairs stayed on the door until they peeled off in the damp, and the wind finally got rid of them. But the officers had proper posters printed, and stuck about the town; they had the dirt and the dead flies cleaned out of the gas lamp over the entrance and set it flaring away so that the whole place came to life; and they even got a London actress to come down and take one of the women's parts. Nothing like it, for excitement, had ever happened in Billington before.

Squashed into a seat at the back of the gallery I saw the whole show, and could have sat through it a hundred times, it was so ravishing. There was one scene whose beauty made the heart stand still. A girl sat in the middle of the stage, lit up by a beam of coloured light from up in the roof. She sang a song, about how much she loved somebody, and how far away he was. Then the coloured light on her faded, until it was like a mist; and a strong beam of white light lit up the back of the stage; and there was a man, in a splendid uniform, standing with his arms outstretched, and singing as he slowly moved toward her. It was the lover she had been thinking about. Her voice had been sad till then, but now she stood up and sang in a way that showed how surprised and glad she was, and his song was clear and masterful; and they came together in each other's arms, and patches of coloured light surrounded them and darted about all over the stage like big bright birds. It was a wonder out of wonderland, and left you with a passionate longing for more of this magical world of light and music and make-believe that was so much lovelier than life. Two of the people who had been on before, with a comic act, came up and stood behind me in the gangway. The one nearest me said, 'Jonesy Boy isn't bad in that, if he didn't sing flat all the time.' The other one said, 'The only decent thing about that old routine was the lights.' I expect they were jealous, because it got a lot more clapping than they did.

When spring came, and the last of the soldiers moved away, it was easier to see how many of our own people had gone too. By ones and twos they had drifted off to that insatiable war. They came back in their uniforms for leave, and then went overseas, to places no one had ever heard of before, some of them; others were just swallowed up in France; but wherever they went the chances were that they would not come back. Byfield seemed dead and empty, the whole rhythm of its life broken by the war. Even our regular callers, the ones we depended on and whose visits were like a calendar for marking the days, stopped coming. The first to drop off was the insurance agent, who came round on a bike once a week to collect burial money. We used to rely on him to tell us what was going on in the other villages, what potatoes were selling at, and if there was a good crop of plums or apples about and what effect it would have on the price. He got a job in the Brewery office at Billington that paid him better and did his collecting at nights, or when he could, and hadn't any time to stop and talk. Then the baker said we should have to make do with one call a week, because his son had gone to the war and now there was his round to do as well; and the butcher said that if we wanted meat we should have to fetch it, which meant walking up to Keloe. Even Jacky Brill, the drunken fishmonger, stopped erupting on to us, and found something more exciting to do.

His sons must have been very glad, because he was an awful nuisance to them. They were respectable young men. Jacky Brill's visits were irregular, but they brightened us up like flashes of lightning. He really got his living with a fish stall in Billington market, but if he had any stock that was not going to keep much longer, he would go round the villages in the evening and give us a call. By that time he was usually pretty well lit up. He would come, whooping and yelling along the lanes, beating his lathered horse unmercifully with the butt end of the whip, or a stick out of the hedge, or anything he could get hold of; anything to force him along at breakneck speed. He would jerk the poor beast to a standstill in front of some houses, and stagger round to the back of his cart, which the weight of the heavy fish boxes pulled down as if they were going to lift the weary animal off its legs. If he was drunk enough he would let a customer have a dozen bloaters, threaded together with a stick through their eyes, for tuppence or threepence. But even then, decent women didn't like to go out to his cart by themselves, because he would start pulling them about if he had half a chance. Sometimes, when he had practically given his stuff away, one of his sons would come round the next day, and explain the circumstances, and try and get a little more money. Jacky ought to have broken his neck half a dozen times; sometimes he was thrown out of his cart, sometimes he just fell out; but the horse always went on home, and one of his sons would go back and pick him up. After a particularly bad spill he generally turned over a new leaf. Any travelling evangelist who happened to be at one of the local chapels at the time could be sure of having Brother Brill as one of his more dramatic successes. Then he would be sober and quiet for a day or two, and very respectful to his customers. Mrs Driffield herself would have him bring some fish into the rectory kitchen, and tell him how glad she was that he had turned over a new leaf and was going to be a credit to his sons; but the new leaf soon got as tattered and dirty as the old one. Give him a fortnight, or three weeks at most, and he would be as drunk as ever. We missed Jacky as much as anybody. There was always something to talk about when he was around.

Then Mr Mabbet stopped coming. Everybody liked him, and his pony and trap had been a regular sight in the village for thirty or forty years. He was an institution. Two days a week, year in year out, he left his shop in Billington in the care of his daughter, and went round the villages with a pony and trap, selling small things that he carried about with him; and taking orders for suits, and corduroy trousers, lengths of calico or flannelette, or women's things. If you wanted a new cap or a pair of grey woollen stockings or a card of buttons, he would let down the tailboard of his trap and bring out big cardboard boxes full of them, and you could take your pick. This trap was unique, specially built for the job. Mr Mabbet had used it for a good many years and his father had gone about in it before him. There was a comfortable, cushioned seat, with a rail round it, and a mackintosh apron to button over the knees when it was cold or wet. The body of it hung low, with broad, curling mudguards; and, opening at the back, running right forward under the driver's seat, was a deep boot in which he carried his goods. The little brown dumpling of a mare that pulled it about was as well known as her master or the trap. She took him on his rounds during the week, and out to the chapels he went to on a Sunday, for he was a Methodist lay preacher as well as a haberdasher.

Mr Mabbet never hurried her, and whenever he stopped for any length of time he pulled a canvas nosebag out of the boot, from among the caps and the stockings, and gave her something to munch while he was away. He came to Byfield once a fortnight or so, there were a lot of villages to fit in. In the wintertime he might not turn up for a month, then he would say to the customers who had been expecting him, 'I've not been going round much lately, the state the roads are in it's hard on Polly's legs,' and everybody understood at once; because Polly the plump mare and Mr Mabbet were regarded as one. Mr Mabbet was plumpish himself, a short thickset man, with a white beard, cut square. In his shop he always wore a black frock coat, but for his rounds he relaxed into a tweed jacket and a cloth cap. His daughter was cut on the same lines as her father, a little shorter if anything, so that when she was behind the counter, with the fashionable leg-of-mutton sleeves ballooning out, and her profusion of yellow tresses piled in a lofty arrangement on the top of her head, she looked all blouse and hair. She went out with her father on Sundays, and sang solos in the chapels where he preached, and her musical gifts were much appreciated. When you thought of new clothes you thought of Mr Mabbet. Byfield people would have considered anything inferior which was bought somewhere else. Boys especially, for a pair of cord trousers from Mr Mabbet always had sixpence in the pocket. Some thought that Mr Mabbet put it there, others that it was a peculiarity of the make. He always called at our house, whether we had any orders for him or not. Mother had a cup of tea ready for him, and listened to his news; though she wasn't very interested in chapel gossip from anybody else. His talk was generally about the places he had been to on Sundays and how the cause was getting on there, who had died, and any revival meetings that might be coming along, and how the Lord had dealt with him. There wasn't a shade of humbug in his make-up, and somehow that made him worth listening to.

Having a shop and going about the country with a pony and trap was a very good way of getting a living. Pottering round the villages with Polly and the trap, well wrapped up, behind the mackintosh apron if it was wet, jogging comfortably along on fine days, reading a book perhaps. Meeting people, and talking to them. It would be very pleasant if I could only get Mr Mabbet to take me on. But it wouldn't do for me to go and ask him, straight out, if he would give me the job. A revolutionary idea like that would have to be put gently into his head at first so as not to frighten him. Mother was the one to do that. Several times she said to him that he ought not to keep going out in all weathers like he did. Why didn't he get somebody to drive the pony and trap, and do the rounds, so that he could give all his time to the shop, and take care of himself a bit more? At first he seemed quite upset at the idea of giving up; then he began to come round to it, and said that he would have to think it over. 'Perhaps Mabel could take the round. Young women were doing such things now, it was a great change, a great change. No doubt it was due to so many men being away at the war.' But Mother said it was hardly the sort of thing for a young lady to do, being out with a horse and trap, alone on the roads. It was all coming along very nicely. He was about ready for me to ask him if he would take me on, when it all fell through. He decided to give up the round altogether. There was so little to sell, he said, and with so many men away at the war there was not the demand. It was his duty to take care of himself, and keep his health for his Sunday work. So that was that. Mother missed him coming in and talking.

Chapter 17

Mr Stubbs had practically given up the secondhand furniture trade, he only went to his stall now on Saturday nights, and spent all the week at the new munition works. It had blossomed out of a shop that used to supply halters and cart sheets but was making a fortune now out of selling tents and canvas articles of all kinds to the army. Anybody who was not liable to be called up or was not working on the land could get a job there, and the pay was fabulous. Mr Stubbs was earning more than he had ever thought of getting before in his life, but he still sold furniture on Saturday nights; partly because there were so many people who wanted it, now that new things were hard to get, and partly to have something to go back to when the war was over. So I still went into Billington every week; and though there were not many fresh books to look at, or buy, because people who had any to get rid of sent them to the Red Cross, there was one now and then that I wanted, and in any case, I liked talking to Stubbs; it seemed to me now that there was a good deal more in what he said than I used to think. No more Latin books turned up, not that I really wanted any more because the ones I had got were as much as I could manage, but I would have bought more if I had found them; and I was always hoping to come across English translations of those I had. Not finding any, I struggled on with such help as the pencilled-in bits and the notes could give, but without knowing whether the translation I was hammering out was the right one or not. Interest in what I was reading pulled me along. Caesar's battles, and Virgil's poetry, captured me as they had done many thousands, for many centuries; and there was the satisfaction of solving a puzzle, as meaning began to emerge from the chaos of unknown words. But there was more than that. Latin gave me self-respect. Plodding my way through this noble old language, feeling that I was breaking into a secret which brought distinction to those who possessed it, and that I was doing this without the help or even knowledge of others, kindled a pride that was very good for me just then. Where it would lead to, or if it would lead anywhere, I could not tell. What earthly use Latin would be to a farm labourer it was impossible to see; but there was always the hope that a chance of some sort would come, and education, people said, was never amiss; and I liked it, and there was nothing else that was half so interesting to do, and so I went on.

As the stock was sold off and nothing much more came in, trade grew slack of a Saturday night and there was plenty of time for conversation. There was always the war to talk about, and Robert Blatchford. With his straw hat on, his old apron, thick with furniture stain, and a Woodbine dangling from his lips, Stubbs would hold forth, perched on the top of a tall office stool, while I listened to him from a broken-legged easy chair that was too bad for anybody to want. The war had dispersed the little group that tried to hold meetings, so he had nobody else to let his ideas loose on. 'There was another chap from Byfield killed in France last week,' I said. 'His mother has got it into her head that he isn't killed at all, but is coming home. She keeps going to the gate to look for him. She is going melancholy mad.' 'Ah poor soul! Chaps all over England are being killed, and their mothers taking on about it, I daresay.' 'It's a rotten thing, this war.' 'You can say that again, but it will do good just the same. It's going to give the working man the biggest boost he's ever had. It'll be a different country when it's over. We shall have a chance for Merrie England at last; that's to say if we have the guts to see that we get it. It won't come easy, mind you,' he went on, warming to the old subject, 'but everything has been loosened up. The bosses won't ever be able to sit on our backs as they used to do, not ever again. The war has done that. Lloyd George says it is a war to make the world safe for democracy. The men who have fought it will take him at his word. They'll want some of that democracy when they get back.' 'But haven't we got democracy already?' I said. The history books I had been reading told me that it was England's peculiar glory to have a democratic constitution. 'That's what they say. But it will have to be something different to what we have had. Working men in politics, more education, better chances for everybody, that's what has got to come. When we have working men in politics we'll have nationalisation, so that we can run the country on the profits of the country's labour, instead of letting the profiteers suck it all up. We'll do away with taxes. It's bound to come.' 'Do you reckon we shall ever see all that?' I said doubtfully. 'A proper education for everybody, I mean?' It was the idea of as much education as anybody wanted being available for anybody that sounded attractive. Running the country without taxes seemed a bit advanced. 'Aye, we shall see it all right. We are dead down here, but up North the unions know what they want, and they will get it too. Young chaps like you will have to stick up for theirselves. Look at the miners!' The only miner I had ever looked at was Arthur, dying so uncomplainingly in my bed.

'This war is a different kind of war than we have ever had before,' he went on. 'It used to be "fight to beat the French", or "fight to put the Boers in their place". Then, when the working man had done it, because he is the one that does the fighting, not these general chaps, it was "thank you very much, and here is a medal, and we don't want you any more." But this is fighting for democracy; that is something we can see we get.' 'Do you think this war will go on much longer, George?' I said, putting the question everybody was asking. 'The sort of generals we've got, it could go on for ever,' he answered, dripping pessimism. 'They haven't woke up. They don't know it's a different kind of war. They used to say, "There is the enemy, men. Charge!" That is about all the generals had to do, so that is all they can think of now. Sending men to charge through all that mud, to attack machine guns! Somebody will have to answer for that, when the war is over. But it is a good thing in its way, mind you. It has shown up a lot of things. All that gup they used to stuff us up with! You won't get anybody to believe in it, after this. They've been had too much. The biggest fool alive won't trust what the upper classes say again. We will do our thinking for ourselves, and it won't be what they like. God Almighty's chosen rulers!' he commented, with ineffable scorn. 'You won't get a two-year-old to swallow that. It's us now. We will do away with poverty.

We'll have justice between man and man. That is what we will have. Robert Blatchford's ideas will get a chance. You will see!' 'Funny you can't get justice, without all this. Chaps being killed. All that destruction,' I said, my mind running on the poor, half-crazy woman peering up and down the road from her garden gate for the son who would never come again. But George wasn't thinking of individuals just then, he was thinking of the cause. 'I expect folks need a shake-up, to make them look at things, to make them see what's what. They have had a shake-up now, all right,' he added with a grim chuckle. 'It'll teach them to take things into their own hands a bit more.' 'That's all very well, but how can working people run things, they haven't the experience?' I asked doubtfully. 'Then we shall have to get it. Education is what we want. It is the only way out of the trap. We have been fooled, because we were ignorant. We won't be ignorant any longer. It's chaps like you that we want. Chaps that can pick it up!' This was flattering, but it was not easy to see how it could work out. 'I don't know,' I said modestly, but pleased nonetheless. 'I haven't got any real education. Just a bit of reading here and there. It wouldn't be of use to anybody.' 'That's what you think. Look at Robert Blatchford. Look what he did! He never had a better start than you. Got his education as he got his living, where he could. But he has made this country sit up and take notice. Socialism today would be nowhere without him. A man that has got an education can always pull his weight, wherever he is.' All an ignorant but ambitious man's belief in learning was in his voice. 'Do you remember when I came in and bought that first book? You didn't hold much with books then, George.' 'Well, I was fed up with them being about the place, and that's the truth, and poetry and such may not be of any use to anybody; but the sort of thing Robert Blatchford writes about, the state of the people, economics, that is the stuff.' 'There is a lot about literature and poetry in Blatchford's *Clarion*, George,' I said, just to stick up for the things that pleased me so much, but still I resolved to read about the state of the people, and economics, if I got the chance. 'I think I shall give up this racket after the war and stay on at the works,' he said, waving his hand towards the few sticks of dilapidated furniture that remained. 'They say they are going to keep it on as a factory. The workers will have to be organised. Form a union.' He said this grandly, as if he personally had already formed it, and was proud of the job.

I resolved that should be my future too. As soon as the war was over, and I could get away from the land, I decided I would get a job in the factory and help George with his union. He was right enough, something would have to be done. It wasn't a fair world, however you looked at it. It did need a change. Some understanding of what life must have meant to a person like my mother began to come to me. She was sensitive to things, she had brains, and courage, and all that; yet life had put her through the mangle. She had been squashed between the rollers of poverty and class. Class had ordained that she should be poor, poverty had seen to it that she should never escape from her class. I could see how nice it must be to think that the poor are either fools or failures. They couldn't be bettered, so there was no need to try. Yet all the time, if people had only been willing to see what there was to see, they would have to admit that she had been heroic. She had got every scrap out of herself that life had let her get. Only by squeezing herself dry had she been able to survive as a real person, the sort of person she wanted to be. My father, with all his capacity for simple enjoyment, had been allowed next to nothing to enjoy. His easy, open nature which accepted everything that came, and contrived to wring some drops of satisfaction out of the harshest circumstances, had been chilled and limited in every direction. There was something wrong in a world that let that happen. I couldn't get worked up about the squire and the parson, as George did sometimes. They had done their best to make the system tolerable; it was the system itself that was wrong. The framework of society, in which we all had to live our lives, needed to be changed. So I decided that I would get work in the factory, as soon as I could, and help George with his union for a start, and see what happened then.

I was working now with Eli and the cows all the time, and liked it better than anything I had ever done. With so much extra land under plough, it was no use going about it with horses. A contractor came with a steam plough and ripped up three or four fields in no time. John had gone off to the war. He put his age on a bit and nobody asked any questions; they had stopped being as particular as all that at the recruiting office, and Mother was not the one to stop him if he wanted to, it would come to that in the end anyway. If the war lasted very much longer I should have to go too, and it looked as if it was going on for ever. There was nobody left on the farms now but old men and boys and a few crocks, and these new-fashioned land girls, that went round in breeches and gaiters like men, and scandalised old people by standing about with their hands in their breeches pockets. We hadn't any of them at Lower House Farm, Johnson didn't need them. The horse dealing had stopped, Eli and I could manage the milking, and Spicer and Barky Britnell spent all the winter round the yards, fattening stock. Our paths never crossed, so I had nothing more to do with Spicer; but he took his bad temper out on Barky, the more so because he had never forgotten the row they had when Barky saved me from being knocked about with the plough paddle. There was hardly a day when he didn't drive the poor old man into one of his gibbering rages. He took pleasure in it, it was an amusement; but he was careful not to do it when Johnson or Eli were about or when I could get at him; hard work in the open air, and a couple of years' growth, had made me his equal.

I was up on a hayrick one morning, cutting out the fodder for the cows in great wads with the heavy, broad-bladed hay-knife, when I saw Spicer up to one of his tricks again. He and Barky were clearing out the yard, Spicer throwing muck to Barky, and Barky tossing it over the wall. Two forksful out of three, Spicer threw so that the filth went all over the old man. Barky was dodging about, and swearing, and getting in a rage, but being plastered with muck just the same. It was rare fun for Spicer. Suddenly I saw him do it. Barky's back turned, for an instant, with the swing of his throw, and Spicer deliberately lunged forward and pricked Barky on the behind with the sharp tines of his dung fork. Barky swung round, pain, surprise and frantic rage convulsed him. He struck, and struck, and struck again at Spicer who never had time to lift an arm, or do anything, but went down, stunned beneath the blows. What last few shreds of a rational mind the poor old man possessed had been tormented out of him by Spicer's dirty tricks in the last half hour; and that final jab with the fork had swept away all consciousness of what he was doing in a burst of frenzy. He bashed and bashed away at the prone body until the blood came and Spicer lay still. I slid down the ladder with my heart in my mouth. It was murder! It must be! Barky's rage broke in a fit of trembling as I caught him and wrenched the fork from his hands. Spicer was not dead, though his head was streaming with blood, and he was unconscious. He had asked for it, and he had got it, but that did not make things any better. It was lucky that Barky was as mad as he was – a saner man, in such a rage, might have stabbed with the fork instead of bashing with it, and then Spicer would have been dead without a doubt.

We laid him on a hurdle and took him home, Eli and I. His wife was a solid woman, only interested in ducks, she wasn't afraid of him. All she said when we brought him in, battered and bloody, was, 'So he has been done in, has he? I told him he would get it one of these days. Lay him on the floor a minute, till I get something to put over the bed. I'm not having him muck up my clean quilt.' Then the police came. Moxon, our constable, had sent for the sergeant from Billington, who asked a lot of questions. The sergeant was a cautious man, he gave nothing away; but kept on asking this and that, and writing the answers down in his notebook, stopping now and then to sharpen his pencil, and being very careful to get a good point on it. When he had finished with me he sent for Barky; but he was wasting his time. He could get no sense out of him at all. The sight of police uniforms drove the bedraggled little man into a petrified silence. The sergeant gave it up. 'Here, you see what you can get out of him,' he said to Moxon disgustedly. But the local man could do no better. 'Well, I never did see such a chap,' said the sergeant, shutting up his notebook. 'It's my belief he ought to be put away somewhere. He'd be better took care of somewhere than left to go about knocking people over with muck forks. He could do with it by the look of him.'

Barky was trembling with terror as he watched the policemen go away. By evening he had pulled himself together, and had got as much of his wits back as he ever had; even then, he slunk into our house like somebody with bloodhounds on his trail. 'It's the police, Mrs Hillyer, they are after me,' he said, scared through and through. Mother sat him down by the fire and gave him some tea. 'The police are after me,' he said again. 'They think I killed Harry Spicer.' 'I don't wonder at the police being after you, the way you've been carrying on,' said Mother, being sharp for his own good, the way she could be at times. 'But you needn't worry about Harry Spicer, he ain't killed. His head's too thick for that. But they'll have you up in court I expect. Now what did you do it for?' It was not so much a query as a remonstrance. 'I never meant to hit him, Mrs Hillyer. He jabbed me with that fork, and I swung round, and there he was, laughing. And then he was down on the ground bleeding.' He was piteous in his effort to make her understand. 'Well, if that's all it was, they can't do a lot to you for that. Harry Spicer is no good. Plenty of people have promised to give him a meeting. It would have been better for you if they had. It might have taken him down a peg. Now you stop worrying. Come on now, have your tea. And don't you go hitting people with forks, even if they do give you a bit of a jab sometimes.' Poor Barky wilted even more under what he thought was her displeasure. She was handling him in what she took to be the best way. Telling him that nothing serious would come of it, to cheer him up a little, but trying to impress him with the enormity of hitting people, in case he got a habit of it. It was the way she would have talked to a child. 'That sergeant said I ought to be put away,' he said, coming to his supreme fear. 'They won't put me away, will they, Mrs Hillyer?' 'Not if you behave yourself they won't, but if you go about hitting people they will.' The thought of being put away was bringing on his excitement again. 'I ain't going to be put away. I be all right where I be,' he stammered out, struggling to make the words come plainly, his face working, his eyes wild. 'If they send anybody to get me I'll kill 'em.' 'Now then, that's enough of that!' said Mother sharply. 'You be in trouble enough as it is without talking about killing people. If that policeman was to hear you now, he'd have you locked up, that he would, right away. Now you sit still,' seeing that he was getting more and more agitated. 'Nobody won't do anything to you if you behave yourself; but if you threaten people they will have to lock you up. They have got to keep the peace.' He quieted down a little, just muttering to himself, 'I ain't going to be locked up. I ain't going to let anybody lock me up,' his words trailing away into a sort of moan, as if, in spite of his defiance, he felt himself helpless before the threat. The trembling old man sat there in his stinking rags, still foul with the muck that had been flung over him; his hands, caloused with work and grime, wrapped round the teacup as if he was wringing some feeble sense of security from so familiar a thing. Shaggy, disreputable, disconsolate, fright and confused anger churning about in him; more than fifty years of ill usage concentrated itself into this one vast fear and beat at his heart.

'Now don't you think about it any more,' said Mother, in as soothing a tone as she could manage. 'You get a good night's rest, and it will all look different in the morning. Nothing ain't happened to you yet, and nothing ain't going to happen.' It was the best she could do. She had never learned how to put her kindness into words; and now that she sought for some phrase, some turn of thought, which might carry a little peace with it, she could find nothing better than this. Father smoked and said nothing. What could any of us say? Mother got up briskly and started to clear the table. Suddenly she said, 'I think you had better stop here tonight. I can make you up a bed by the fire. And you had better get washed too, that muck you got on you stinks something awful.' Perhaps it was the washing that put him off, or something in his muddled mind that we could not grasp; but he shuffled, uneasily, out of his chair, and said, 'Thank you very much, Mrs Hillyer. I be grateful. But I got to get back. I got to get back. I be going home.' He put his old bowler hat on, and edged away towards the door, slipping out as if he thought we might force him to stay if we noticed that he was going. 'It might be a good thing for him to be put away in a sort of a home. They would keep him clean,' said Father as he went. 'Keeping clean ain't everything,' answered Mother surprisingly.

It was getting on for ten o'clock. Mother had gone up to bed, Father was laying out the sticks and paper all ready for lighting the fire in the morning. 'Are you going to be long?' he asked. 'About half an hour,' I said, turning over a page of Virgil to look at the place I had marked as the end of my stint for that day. 'Well, I won't wait then. You lock up, and put out the lamp.' He was half asleep already. There was a knock at the door, and he paused, on his way to the stairs, to open it, grumbling, 'Now who is this, at this time o' night?' Gwen Potter stood there, outlined against the dark. 'My grandad says Mrs Hillyer has got to come and stop Barky Britnell,' she bolted out, shrill with the importance of her message. 'He is hollering about in the chapel something dreadful. My grandad says if you don't stop him he will send for the police.' The chapel was at the back of the Pheasant, quite close. 'Mrs Hillyer has gone to bed, but I'll come myself, in half a minute, when I get my shoes on,' answered Father, puzzled. I shut up the book and went with him. 'Now how the nation did he get into that chapel?' he said as we went up the lane; it was chilly after the warmth of the house. 'He will get hisself into trouble, do what you may. He will be setting the place alight, I shouldn't wonder.' 'He ain't in the chapel,' said Gwen, contradicting what she had just said. 'Not in the chapel, really. He is in that place at the back, where he chops the wood.' 'Oh, is he?' said Father, relieved. 'There ain't no call to bother then. He is allus in there.' 'But he is hollering, Mr Hillyer, hollering like anything, and throwing things about.' Gwen sounded scared. 'I don't hear nothing now,' said Father, as we got near the place. 'Perhaps he has had enough of it and gone home,' I said. 'Well, we had better have a look and see, now that we are here. Hullo, he has got a light in there. I said he will be setting the place afire, and he will too.' I remembered that Barky had a reputation that way. Father pushed at the door. Something swinging knocked against it as it opened. There was a dark shape, hanging from a beam, with ragged trouser legs and dirty boots at the end of it; swaying as if the door had just set it in motion. 'My God, he has hung hisself!' Father shouted. He lifted the dangling body up in his arms, while I sawed at the rope with my knife. The bit of candle, guttering away, gave next to no light, and the rope was tough. It parted at last, and we laid the body down on the floor. He was still warm, limp and very skinny. You could feel the bones like hard ridges under his rags. 'You had better cut off for the doctor, Dick,' said Father, in an awed voice.

It was half an hour before I got to the doctor, though I ran best part of the way. He didn't seem too pleased at my banging and thumping on the door at that hour of the night. It opened with a jerk. 'Now then, what is all this racket about?' 'It's Barky Britnell, sir, he has hung himself.' 'Did you walk up here?' 'Yes sir, I come as quick as I could, across the fields.' 'If he has been dead that time, there is no need for hurry. They have cut him down, I suppose?' The doctor got out his horse and trap, and I helped him. Willie Potter was there in the chapel shed, and three or four more besides. Somebody had brought a lantern, and they had covered the body with an old sack. The doctor stooped, and turned it back, feeling gently beneath the rags; then he held his watch for a moment before the distorted lips, but no sign of breath dimmed it. He pulled the sack over the still form again and got up. We waited for the doctor to settle what we knew already. 'Well,' he said, 'he is dead. You had better let Constable Moxon know, and fetch Mrs Bone while you are at it.' Outside, in the starlight, he stood feeling absently for a cigarette, and looking at his horse and trap in the way people see things when they are thinking of something else. 'He hadn't anybody, I suppose, poor devil?' he said, as he threw away the match. 'No sir, not a soul.' 'Well, Constable Moxon will see to it,' and he drove off.

It was a strange parson that took the funeral, the Rector was away. Selina Vear talked about letting Barky's cabin to anybody who wanted it, but nobody did, and it soon fell down. I looked in after a week or two, but it was already mouldy and rotten. There was a feeling about the place as if it was haunted by misery, by the ghost of despair, when despair itself was dead. I took away his hunting picture, I thought Barky would like that saved. It had been something he liked, and there had not been many of them – chapel, perhaps, and chopping wood in the shed where he died, the red rapture of fire, and Mother's sharp kindness. I wished now that I had done something for him. If I had tried I might have broken his isolation a little. He had been shut up in it, walled round with hunger, loneliness, fear and a hostile world. Even as a child he could have known very little else. All his life, thrashing about in the dark of his mind, there had been Old Arnison, always there, never to be shaken off. Nobody to trust, nobody to help him, except Mother, and she, in spite of trying, had been no use when he wanted help most. Most likely he had got it into his muddled head that she too wanted him shut up. So he had gone to the shed at the back of the chapel, driven by the same instinct which drives a hunted animal to a place where it has known safety; but there was nothing for him even there but a frenzy of fear, impotent rage and death. Until then he had lived by the sheer momentum of life, by that force which keeps a man going on, simply because he is going on. And then it failed. The intolerable weight suddenly broke him, and he crashed down into the darkness. But was it darkness? Barky had been a good chapel man, he believed in the next world. Perhaps, when he put the rope round his neck, he thought that he was taking a desperate short cut to that goodness which would lift him up, and look after him at last. However hopelessly he had lived, he might have had hope when he died. Yet all those things that he had been forced to put up with had not all been deliberate cruelty. Most of the people who had plagued him had never thought that they were doing much harm, they were just having a bit of fun with old Barky. Johnson, who had paid him barely enough to keep him breathing, had thought that he was doing a kindness, of a sort, to a mad old man who was too big a risk for anybody else to employ. No, they had not all been cruel all through. Only two of them. For Arnison and Spicer the hottest hell wouldn't be hot enough. There had got to be a hell for people like that.

Chapter 18

Mother had got something on her mind; I could see that the minute I got in from work, something that pleased her too, by the look of things. All teatime I could see that she was saving something up. It was no use pushing her when she was like that, she would get round to it when she was ready. She had been mending my old Latin dictionary, because it was beginning to drop to pieces, what with age and the use it had been getting lately. Anything like that she did to a miracle, she was the neatest person at mending anything that you ever saw. It was lying there ready for me on the chest-of-drawers, strong and tidy again. 'The Rector has been here this afternoon,' she said at last, with the air of a person making an important disclosure. 'Has he? It's not his day is it?' I said, without much interest. He was always as regular as Sunday in his visits, and one wasn't due for another week. 'No, but he has just got back, and he wanted to hear about poor Barky. He was put out by all that trouble with Harry Spicer and the suicide and everything that happened while he was away. He was quite upset about it.' There was a pause, and then she came out with it. 'He wants you to go over and see him tonight.' 'What is the good of my going over there, I can't tell him anything more than you can. I told you what happened in the yard, and round at the chapel.' 'It isn't about Barky.' 'What is it then?' I said, irritated at her playing at mysteries like this.

'Well, I was mending your book when he came in. He has never caught me so untidy before. There was paste and paper clippings and I don't know what, all over the table. So when he had sat down and I had told him about Barky, he said, "I see you are mending a book, Mrs Hillyer. You seem to have done it remarkably neatly. May I look at it?" So he picked it up. I could see he was surprised. "A Latin Dictionary, Mrs Hillyer! May I ask whose it is?" Then I told him it was yours, and he said, "Can he understand it?" And I said, "Oh yes, he uses it a lot, that is why it is dropping to pieces. He has got some more books of the same kind, upstairs." So I took him up, and showed him the ones you have got in your bedroom. He was up there twenty minutes, I should think. He kept taking books out, and looking at them, and saying, "Does he really read all these?" He wanted to know where you got them from, and I said you bought them in Billington Market. He was fair surprised! It put Barky Britnell right out of his head, and he was full of him when he came. He kept saying, "And does he really read all these, Mrs Hillyer?" and I said you did, and he said you were to go over to the Rectory at eight o'clock tonight, when he has finished his dinner, because he wants to talk to you about it.' So that was it. Now it was all out, and she was thrilled.

But it shook me rather. I wasn't expecting anything like it. I didn't know whether to be glad or sorry. There had been times when I had wondered whether it would be any good to talk to Mr Wickens or the Rector, and see if anything came of it, but I couldn't make up my mind. As far as the schoolmaster was concerned, he might help or he might not. He hadn't been too keen about the scholarship. He might listen, or he might not. He would probably say, 'Yes, yes, very praiseworthy,' or something like that, and then do nothing about it; and of course it would get all over the village that I had been to Wickens, to get him to send me away to college, and he had turned me down, and I should look a bigger fool than ever. As far as the Rector was concerned, it was a pretty big jump to go and talk to him about things like that. I didn't know how he would take it. He was decent as a rule, but this was different. It was aiming pretty high, and he might not like it. And hanging about at the back of my mind was the idea that it looked like begging, and I could not bring myself to that. So I did nothing about it. With a curious kind of guarded feeling that anything might happen, and it might or might not be what I wanted; and that in any case I would not say too much until I was sure that I was going to get a fair hearing, I went through the little door in the garden wall, and along the winding path between the espalier apple trees to the side door, which village people were expected to use. I had gone that way hundreds of times before, only tonight the dark shapes of the trees, the feel of the path beneath my feet, the earthy smell of the garden, seemed unfamiliar, and to have a meaning that I could not catch.

They only had one maid at the rectory now, owing to the war, and it was Miss Lucy herself who opened the door and took me along the passage to Mr Driffield's study, chattering all the way. He was lying back in a long easy chair, smoking a pipe, and didn't look particularly hospitable. There was a mahogany chair with a horsehair seat placed in front of him, and he motioned to me to sit there, and went on smoking, as if he had not decided yet what he was going to do with me. The room was oppressively quiet, the horsehair cold and slippery. He took his pipe out of his mouth, held it in his hand, looking at it for a minute, and then said, 'I called at your mother's this afternoon and she showed me some books of yours. Tell me about them.' 'Tell you what, sir?' 'Well, how you got them, and what put you on to reading them.' So I told him about Mr Stubbs, and the stall in the market, and going into Billington on Saturday nights to get them; but I couldn't have told him what the books had meant to me, even if I had wanted to. 'And the Latin?' he said. 'How did that come about?' So I told him. 'And you really have been teaching yourself all this time and said nothing to any of us about it? Well, we must find out what you know.' I could see what was in his mind. Granny was cropping up again. Just because she had taken a short cut to what she wanted to be – imagined herself a lady – he thought that I might be doing much the same sort of thing. That I had got hold of some Latin books and pretended to myself that I was a scholar, and could read them.

He asked me some simple grammar questions at first, and then went on to harder ones. That wasn't difficult because I knew good old Henry by heart and just spouted what I had learned. He was getting interested. He got up, went to his desk, and wrote down a few sentences in Latin and English; then he called me over and said, 'See if you can translate these.' They were not too hard, either. So I put down what I thought they might be and gave him his paper again. This time he was definitely interested. He read what I had written, marked one or two places, put the paper down and paused. Now, I thought, it is coming, the real test. He walked over to the bookshelves, which ran all round the room, reached up to the corner of one of them and took down a volume, while I watched him. He laid it on his desk, flicked through the pages for a moment, and fixed on a passage. 'There,' he said, with his finger on a particular line, 'you have been reading Caesar you say, see if you can translate that.' It was the passage in the first book of the Civil Wars, in which Caesar tells how he moved his troops to Rimini, crossed the Rubicon and so settled his future for ever. I think the whim occurred to him that this should be my Rubicon, if I could do that he would take me seriously. For the first time the hope sprang up in me that there might be a way out at last, that if he liked what I did, that if I could convince him that I had accomplished something and had the power to do more, he might help me; and there would be an end to drudging about on a farm, and I might have a chance to make the kind of future for myself that I wanted. I stumbled into a translation. It was crude and bald, a coherent sentence was hard to make. If I had been at home it would have straightened itself out all right, I daresay, but here, in my eagerness to impress him, it was jumbled and broken. 'Take it quietly,' he said. 'There is no hurry,' and the cool voice, with a note of kindness in it for the first time, steadied me, and the words began to come in better order, until I had finished the paragraph.

He made no comment, but shut the book, and stood for a minute looking down at it. The lamp on his desk lit up the two of us, and the closed book, which had a coat of arms stamped on its polished leather cover. The moment held my fate. All the shadows round seemed waiting, as I was waiting, for what he would say. 'I think I owe you an apology, my boy. You can do it. I didn't expect it, but you can. Sit down, and let us see where we go from here.' The arrangement was that he would give me an hour, after dinner, two nights a week. As soon as he saw that the Latin was not too bad he started me on Greek. He made no promises, and no comments, apart from teaching me what I needed to know; but when the lesson was over he would chat about books, about the literature and history I had read; and I saw that he was probing round to discover whether I really had read the books I had collected, and how much I understood of them.

When this had been going on for about six months, he said one night, 'Well, Richard, it is time we began to think of the future. It seems to me, from what I can see of you, that you may have a genuine gift as a classic. The thing is, what are we to do with it? That is the problem. A lot depends on how hard you want to work, but there might be a way. I don't say it will come off, but we can try. You have got to get to a university. Now I understand from a friend of mine, who teaches there, that Durham University has some scholarships that might be within your reach. Would you like to try for one?' Would I like to try! It was as if heaven had opened, and the golden city had dropped right down at my feet, with all its doors wide open. 'Well, they sit in July, but you won't be ready this year. It will have to be next, and then, if the war is still on, you will probably be in the army; but we must hope for the best and plan for next year.' Next year was all right with me, any time, provided I got a chance. He saw my excitement, and started damping it down. 'It will be slavery for the next few months, if you are going to do it. You've a long way to catch up.' But who cared about slavery!

The next week Mr Driffield gave me a job in his garden. It was just an excuse for me to have some wages to take home to my parents while I gave most of my time to study. Every morning he gave me two hours' coaching, then I could take as much time as I wanted for the work he set me; and if there was any time left, I filled it in doing whatever Miss Lucy set me about the flower-beds. It was fantastic! All day for study, and the harness room to myself to do it in. A place of my own, to be alone in! I slaved away there, only stopping at night when the light that came through the little window above the door was no longer sufficient to see by. Then to sit there, quietly happy, looking at the sky, which was all there was to see. Clouds, splashed with sunset colours, opening and shutting, scenes building up and falling apart; great shapes, moving like figures in a distant drama, vague and mysterious; then curtains swing together and they are hidden, and everything dissolves into the dark.

Of course the people in the village were talking. Mr Bilbee stopped me one day, and hummed and hawed a bit, and said, 'So you are going to be a scholar, Richard, quite a scholar! Now that is a very fine thing indeed. I thought of trying for the regular ministry myself once, but it was not the Lord's will. I wish it had been. A great work, the ministry! You will be having a go at it yourself, one of these days, eh?' I said I did not know, and I didn't. The future could take care of itself, only the present mattered. Mr Stubbs looked like a man who felt that he had been taken in but wasn't surprised, because life was like that. 'Well, there goes another good man,' he said. 'You won't be interested in the cause now. Every man for himself.' I felt peeved at his mistrust. 'Why not?' I said. 'I shall be more use to the cause with an education than without; you said yourself that education was what was needed!' 'Not the sort you will get at Durham University, Latin and Greek and all that stuff. It's only good for parsons and schoolteachers. If you were going to study something useful, like economics, and the state of the people, it would be different.' 'Well, I might at that, but it has got to be Greek and Latin now, it's the only way I can get in.' 'Good luck to you then. I hope you bring it off,' he said, unbending a little. 'I've got a regular job at the factory myself. I'm starting in a week from now.' I was sorry the old stall was going, I owed it a lot. Mr Wickens got hold of me after church one Sunday, and made me go home with him to supper, and pumped me about what I was studying with the Rector, and how it all started, and seemed genuinely pleased that it had come about. He said nothing about that scholarship idea of his that had fallen through. I think he felt bad about it, but was glad that a chance had come along after all.

From just being an oddity, that nobody took much notice of, I was getting quite popular in some quarters, not in all. There were people who said to their neighbours, 'That boy of Bob Hillyer's is sucking up to the parson now, I hear. You mark my words, he will come a cropper, that boy. You can't make a silk purse out of a sow's ear.' And the neighbour would say, 'It's in the family. Look what happened to his granny. He'll go the same way, I shouldn't wonder.' Mrs Blore had me in to tea, I had never had a bite of anything in her house before, in spite of all the times I had been in and out; but now it was a special tea, in the drawing-room, with plates on little tables by our sides, and napkins, and things handed round. 'Now, Richard,' she said, 'when you get your scholarship, as I am sure you will, because the Rector says you are very clever, you will be mixing with better-class people, and you will have to speak and behave as they do.' It was the first time I had heard that Mr Driffield thought me clever. He never told me so. 'So you mustn't be annoyed if I try to help you in a few little ways. There is a right way and a wrong way of speaking, for instance. It will help you if you learn the right way. When you are talking to me, I shall tell you when you go wrong, but you mustn't mind. It's to help you.' I wasn't likely to mind, because I knew well enough that the broad dialect I had spoken all my life wouldn't do out of Byfield. Nobody wants to look a fool, if they can help it. She was a good soul really, and was afraid she might have hurt my feelings, so she went on buttering me up. 'I always thought that you would do something extraordinary, since I discovered that you read Sir Walter Scott. And all those books I lent you! And you never said you were improving yourself all the time!' I wasn't ashamed of my home or my parents, or my dialect, for that matter. But there was no harm in learning to speak correctly, and I would be a fool not to try. Good manners I would trust to myself for.

Katie Blore was a young woman now, still with that odd

look of being somewhere else all the time. In spite of her thick glasses I thought her attractive. She came home from London most weekends. She was different from any girl I had ever seen; except, perhaps, that girl who sang among the dancing lights at the officers' concert, the first winter of the war. I expect I ought to have fallen in love with Katie, in the distant, worshipping sort of way that would have suited the poetry and the books I read; but I didn't, I was too full of myself just then. But I liked Katie a good deal. The weekends were always better and pleasanter when she was at home. Sometimes, when she thought I wasn't looking, I would catch her watching me out of the corners of her eyes; curious to see what the freak was really like, I suppose; but you could never be sure what she was thinking, those thick glasses hid any sign of what was passing in her mind. When she felt like it she would wander over to the piano and start playing, taking no notice of me. I was glad when she did that because I liked to listen to her. The music brought back the hot summer, when I used to catch bits and pieces of what she was playing while I pumped water for her mother's garden. Now I could listen to it all through, sitting in the same room, accepted, in a sort of way, as the kind of person such music was for. If I asked her she would tell me about the pieces she played, who wrote them, and what to listen for, and things like that. She never enthused about anything, just told me as much as I was likely to understand, and let it go at that. At teatime, Mrs Blore would make me hand round the cakes and things as a sort of social training; but she never left us alone together, not even when we were both working in the same place in the garden.

I didn't set much store by the lessons in polite behaviour, but I liked being with Katie. If I was lucky with the scholarship I should probably meet a lot more girls like her. I didn't think that either she or her mother were interested in me personally. So far as they were concerned I was just young Hillyer, a queer sort of farm boy who had brains, whom they were helping; partly because it showed that they could recognise merit even in the oddest places, and partly because what I was doing was a bit of a sensation in the village and Mrs Blore couldn't keep out of it.

In November the war was over, and the prospect of being called up for the army disappeared. It was settled that I should sit for a scholarship in the following July, and the entry went in. Mr Driffield thought that I stood a chance, but not more. The Latin was not bad, but there was still a long way to go in Greek, and I would need a lot of luck. There was an English and a Divinity paper to do as well, and there was no time for any special work on them, they would have to be taken as they came, and might beat me. There was no reason to be cock-a-hoop, the whole thing might be a dismal flop, and there were times when I thought that it was pretty sure to be. Still, I would try. The war had skimmed the cream of the schools too soon, and they would not be sending up the usual kind of candidate. Some youngsters who had been lucky and got wounded early on, so that they could go back to their studies, might be putting in for it; still, the competition would be nothing like what it would have been in normal times. I had a chance.

John was billeted at a farm in France and was enjoying

himself helping with the horses, though he had learned about motor-cars in the army and was going to work in a garage when he was demobilised. Father had a notion that I had turned out to be a clever chap, and he was glad about it, though he found all these different goings-on a bit puzzling – John going to work in a garage, Lord Postern talking about selling his land because there wasn't any money in it any more, and me going to college. The war had made a change and no mistake! Still, he was glad about me going to college, and he hoped that John would make out in the garage, and that work like that would be healthy for him. Mother, as usual, was more difficult to understand. When I first told her about Mr Driffield's offer to help me she was quite excited, but it began to fade away after a bit. She kept up a show of being pleased, but it wasn't convincing. She seemed almost worried. I could guess a part of what was in her mind. Life had been too rough with her. She couldn't face anything good without suspecting it. She was looking for the catch, there had to be one somewhere, to her way of thinking. If the Rector had offered to get me a job in an office somewhere she would have taken it better; that would have been something within bounds, something she could believe in. But this idea of going to a university was away beyond anything she could have thought of, and it would take time for her to accept it as possible.

It was a chilly evening for July, and we were sitting by a wood fire in the half-light she liked best. The next morning I would be on my way to Durham, where I was to stay with the Rector's friend, Mr Boddington, while I took the exam. Suddenly she said, 'It's funny how things turn out. If it hadn't been for poor Barky dying like that, you might never have had this chance. If there hadn't been all that to-do, with the Rector away and all, and his coming down that day to find out about it and catching me on the hop like that, he would never have seen the book, and then it would never have started.' 'I don't know. It might have come about in another way. You never can tell,' I answered, a bit resentfully. Why had she got to bring that up? The thought of that squalid body, lying so still in the lantern light, jarred just then, when I was full of what the next few days were going to bring. Still, she was right, in a way. Life given by the dead! A new beginning for me out of Barky's wretched end! A bit melodramatic perhaps, put like that, but there was some truth in it nonetheless. We were quiet for a minute. Then she said, hesitantly, as if she didn't want to say it but it had to come out, 'Will it be all right, Richard, do you think, if you get this scholarship? I mean you won't be out of place? All the rest of them chaps up there will have been brought up to it. Do you think you will be happy in that sort of life? Suppose they won't mix, and you have to be just one on your own?' So that was what was on her mind, was it? But what did it matter? I had got over all that sort of thing by now, though it had bothered me a lot at the time when I was thinking of going to the Grammar School. I hadn't wanted to be cold-shouldered by the better-off boys. But I knew better now. If you want anything, you have got to be prepared to pay for it, if you must. Nothing was going to stop me. 'I mean, you won't feel out of place, my dear?' The small touch of affection showed how anxious she was for me. 'No,' I said. 'Why should I be?' 'They may not want our class of people there. The other students, I mean.' All her lifelong fear of exposing herself to any slight was in her voice. 'Why should I care?' I answered. 'They study there, and I want to study. I can get on by myself, if I have to.' After all, these last few years had not exactly been full of friends. Whatever kind of world lay ahead of me, I would find my way about in it by one means or another. What did it matter if other people, with other backgrounds, had come there by other roads? There was no reason why we should dislike each other on that account. But if they wanted to take a high line, they could. I was self-sufficient.

Chapter 19

There was no need for goodbyes when I left the next morning; after all, I should be back in a day or two, when the exam was over; and I was glad that there was no particular fuss, because I was keyed up at the thought of the journey, and only wanted to get away quietly. Mother came to the door with me, making sure that I had got everything, and then stood watching until I was out of sight down the lane. The last time I saw Katie Blore she said, to my amazement, 'You will let us know how you get on, as soon as you can, won't you?' I did not think that she had taken that much notice. The few people who went by while I was waiting for the bus said, 'Good morning', in a tentative sort of way, as if they were not quite sure where to place me now that I was going away to sit for a scholarship. If I had just been Bob Hillyer's boy, working on a farm like everybody else, they would have stopped to worm out all the details; but this was a new situation, so they were cautious.

Bill Gregory had given up running his horse and van nowadays, there was not enough custom since the bus started. It began during the war, to take people to the munition works; and now they were keeping the factory on, it was going to be permanent. It was an old London bus, adapted to run on coal gas, for petrol was still scarce. It came, billowing along the Billington road, with a half-empty gas bag on its upper deck looking like an expiring balloon that had somehow got entangled with a motor vehicle. Clumsy and fantastic as it was, it spelled the end of the old Byfield; the Byfield that I had been born into, and which had been there since Saxon times, a village which imprisoned and then consumed its own children. Now its inhabitants could move about, and find work and amusement where they wished. They would be a different kind of people, knowing more of good and evil. But when I climbed on board, and took my seat in the ill-devised contraption, which went plunging and rattling along on its solid tyred wheels, I missed the familiar old shambling horse, the slow pace that let you see what was going on in the hedges, and Bill's gossipy curiosity. The bus was in the charge of a perky girl in an overall and peaked cap who was skittish with the young men and supercilious with everybody else.

I had never made a journey by myself before, and apart from that one trip to London had never even been in a train. For the first few hours we went past farms and villages of the kind that I knew. It was comforting, familiar and yet in small ways different, and so was interesting to watch. At Sheffield there was a change of trains, and from there on, as if the train itself belonged to another kind of world, everything else changed. This was something I could never have imagined, a nightmare country, whose grim ugliness was an offence to the spirit; but which still retained, in some overlooked mile or so here and there, a touch of the loveliness it had once displayed, emphasising still more the hideousness of all the rest. The train wound through cuttings, gashed in the dingy rock that was blackened by smoke and steam. It passed grimy factories, piled round with vast heaps of rusty iron. Obscene trickles of filthy water oozed from the buildings and made their way along evil-looking gutters to stagnant ponds that were iridescent with metallic refuse. The train rushed on into a wasteland, blotched with dismal little towns and foundries and railway sidings, jostling one another in their common squalor. This was what industry was like! This was the place where the money was made, the heart of the system which created the wealth we were envied for by the rest of the world. The glory and riches of manufacture, which seemed so splendid in books, came down to this! The reality was harsh as a blow. Mile after mile the train penetrated into this fantastic world. Shabby little rows of houses, with three or four privies at the end, towered over by great pit heaps and the gaunt framework of winding gear. Did they call these places villages? I had been born in a village. Byfield was a village, but it was different from this. Cramped and poverty-stricken though we were, we lived in paradise compared with these festering places. When the sun shone, its light was unhindered by foul miasmas. The air was clean, there were gardens, and pleasant things to see; the land was cared for, and decay itself was only the slow work of time, and had some grace in it. Here all had been ruined from the start by a consuming greed. A blight lay upon everything, the broken fences, the sour, smoke-grimed grass, and the depressed animals that were trying to feed on it.

How could people live in these places, and stay human? These women, hanging out their washing in bleak little back yards, beneath belching factory chimneys; these men in pit clothes, walking home along the muddy paths, what did they think and feel about all this? The children, playing round the slag heaps, what were they growing up to? Were they boxed up in their system, as I had been in mine? If so, they were worse off than I had ever been. How much longer would people, living and working like this, go on putting up with it? They were organised, they were strong, or so George Stubbs said. They would do something some day. Would they be like the Russians, and blow the whole system sky high? Whatever sort of revolution they had, it would be something different from the one George Stubbs thought of, with his Merrie England and Garden of Eden mentality. These would be angry people, and anger can be very cruel. What else could they be but warped and embittered by the things they lived among? My father could be patient, in spite of endless drudgery and poverty, because he dwelt with the vast patience of nature all around him, it moved in the blood of those who spent their nights and days with it. But what had these people got to lighten their lives? Nothing that I could see, except the public houses; the cheap-looking imitation Gothic churches and shabby little chapels with here and there a park or a football ground. There were pigeon lofts at the back of some of the houses, and in one place a group of men were racing whippets on a piece of waste land.

And there were so many of these people. Hundreds of streets of grey-roofed houses snaking up the hillsides in mean little towns and villages, and every house filled with swarming humans, being born, living, dying with nothing but the squalid results of other men's ruthless drive for riches all around them. Some day they would have power. What kind of use would they make of it? What sort of life would they find for themselves, and force on all others? Better than this, certainly, but was there enough kindliness, love and human feeling left among them to make it a gentler world as well? If there were, it would be a very wonderful thing. Or would crude tastes and crude passions, such as were virulent enough to survive in this atmosphere, have their way? The old world was dead, the war had killed it, and a good thing too; the new one that took its place would have to be better, better for ordinary people. It would have to give them better places to live in, better clothes, better things to eat, more education, because that was the only thing that could burst open the prison of class; but nagging away at the back of my mind was the thought that the old world had something good too, loyalties, decencies which I hoped would not disappear altogether. The impact of what I had seen stirred and troubled me. I could think of nothing else. Even when we had passed York, and there was pleasant farming country on either side again, thoughts churned about inside me that blotted out the green fields, and kept me still in that tortured landscape which the train had left behind.

We came out of a cutting on to a lofty viaduct, and there, far below, wound an ancient street. Away to the right, towering above the level of the railway, was a breathtaking sight – Durham Cathedral, that wonder among buildings, riding lordly on its impregnable rock, in the bend of the river, with the castle crouching like a grey old watchdog at its feet; the homely, ancient city – a huddle of slate roofs and weathered brick – pressing up to them for shelter. That first glimpse of Durham is overwhelming in its grandeur. I stood on the platform and stared at it, too fascinated to turn away. I was conscious of somebody stopping beside me. A decent, gentleman's-servant-looking man said, 'It is a very fine view, sir, isn't it? I have been asked to meet you. Mr Boddington is away from home, and I am to look after you.' He picked up my bag. 'If you come with me I will take you to his house. It is quite near, we can walk it in a minute or two. With our hills, it is very often easier to walk.' I went with him. It felt odd to have my bag carried for me, to be walking with a gentleman's servant who talked to me, not as an equal but with a sort of impersonal politeness, which seemed to be something he owed to himself rather than gave to me. We came to a pleasant eighteenth-century house which stood among similar houses in a hilly street that ran along the edge of a steep bank above the river. Opposite to it, on the other side of the stream, were the western towers of that soaring cathedral. The river below was in full spate after recent rain and made a low, steady murmur as it slipped, glass-smooth, over the weir.

A meal was set out for me in a room which had a dark mahogany table, paintings on the walls, a worn carpet with a deep red pattern; and I was helped from silver dishes. It was like living in a book. Everything was clear, and present, and yet unreal. I do not know that I felt out of place. I had read about such houses as this, and imagined them; now it seemed as if I had been lifted bodily out of my old self and put down in some Victorian novel. Mr Boddington's man waited on me with the same aloof politeness which he had shown at the station; if he thought it queer to be waiting on this rough, south-country farm boy he gave no hint of it that I could see. To me it seemed that this was the way civilised people lived, the way I was going to live some day, with luck.

The examination began at ten o'clock the next morning, and I left with plenty of time for the short walk that would take me to the place where it was being held. I was not anxious, it was not that; in a detached sort of way, I was surprised at myself for not being more upset when there was so much at stake; but the whole place was calm, quiet, lovely, and it was good to be out in it that bright morning; walking through the narrow streets, overhearing snatches of conversation carried on in a strong northern dialect that I could barely understand, between women out shopping, old men leaning on sticks, and people calling to one another as they went about their business in the summer sunshine. Across an ancient bridge and up a little street, with a jumble of old shops on either side; then up a steep, cobbled way that brought me out on to a broad place set round with brown stone buildings, ripened by many centuries, and a smooth grass plot in the middle. There was no other human being there but me. A leisurely bell was calling the canons to matins, its sound floating down from the central tower of the vast cathedral, which stood, all light and shadow, in the morning sun. Everywhere there was peace and fulfilment, and the perfection of time's work. The place was like a benediction.

There was an arched gateway, with a lodge on one side of it, where a porter sat reading a newspaper. He nodded as I went past; taking me for granted, as if I belonged to the college, so I hardly liked to ask him the way to the examination room lest I should break that pleasant illusion. The quadrangle, too, was empty. On one side was a flight of steps, leading to a great door that looked as if it was closed for the vacation. A smaller door, further on, stood open as if we were meant to use that; beyond it were some stairs, and at the top of them the college chapel. I went in and said a prayer: the place, the hope and expectation within me supplied the impulse. But there was still the examination room to find, and everything here was deserted. A long gallery, with pictures and statuary on either side of it, looked as if it might lead somewhere, and I went down it. The sound of the canons' bell, through the open windows, had changed now and had a hurrying note, as if it could tolerate lackadaisical ways no longer, for time was short.

The gallery led into a noble hall, with portraits of men in academic dress on the walls, huge polished tables filling the floor; and a gallery, with ancient armour, looking down upon it all. A man in a black tailed-coat ticked my name on a list he carried as I went in, and sent me to a place in the far corner, under the picture of a bearded personage with a globe in front of him, who did not appear to be particularly welcoming. Sitting there, waiting, I could look around. There were fifteen or twenty of us already, and more arriving; some of them were younger than me, but most had the outdoor look of men who had just left the army. One hobbled in with a stick, another had lost an arm. The canons' bell, clear in the hushed room, scampers for a minute, and then stops. There is a pause, nobody knows what to do, the only official present yet is the butler, at the door. Then a plump, red-faced man in gown and bands, carrying a square cap, bustles in and climbs on to the dais, puffing a little as if he has been hurrying to get there in time. He beams on us for a minute, while he gets his breath. His smile is all-enveloping, beginning at the creases in his neck and spreading up into the roots of his hair. Then, in a harsh voice which he strives to make pleasant, he says, 'Gentlemen, you will find this morning's examination papers in a sealed envelope in front of you. You have three hours. You may begin, and good luck!' Like a light, flashing for a second and illuminating some great space before it dies, the thought flooded through my mind as I opened the packet, 'This is it. This is where all the blundering effort, the dreaming, and the luck of the past years has led me; to this room, these papers, and the next few days.' I began to write.

At the end of the week I went home. When the train started, and the great towers slid away and dropped behind me, the elation of the past weeks ebbed out and left me empty and hopeless. What possible chance could I have? I had been a fool to try it. Learning a bit of Latin on my own, as I had done, was all very well, but that didn't make me the equal of these fellows who had been properly taught all their lives. What chance could a raw farm boy have against them? I probably did not know enough to know where I had gone wrong. The papers I had handed in seemed all right, but there might be things behind the questions that I had never guessed at. I had never taken an examination before in my life: all the others had done it plenty of times, they knew the tricks, what to look for. I hadn't a chance. Talking to them, at odd minutes between the papers, most of them seemed pretty sure of themselves. One or two were sitting for scholarships at other places, and would take the best they could get. I hadn't a hope but this: if this failed I should be back where I started, worse off if anything. I should have had my chance and made a mess of it. Everybody would know that I had not lived up to my big ideas, and I would look a fool. I said nothing about the examination, nothing about Durham, when I got home. I did not want to talk about it. Mr Driffield asked me a few questions about the papers, and I told him, but he made no comment. My job at the rectory had come to an end. It had never been a real job, only just an excuse to give me some time for study. I could not expect more help there. So for the next few weeks I hung about home, moody and depressed. Perhaps I would just fail, and never hear anything at all. I had got to do something. There was the factory. They were taking on people, and I could get a job there. George Stubbs would have some help with his union after all, if I didn't make a muck of that, as I had done of everything else.

Then the letter came. The postman did not go by that morning, as he had done on every other morning when I watched for him. A wild pleasure rushed up in me as I read it. I had not failed. I had got a scholarship. Not the best, but one that I could live on, if I was careful and went to one of the less expensive colleges: I had done it! I had broken out of Byfield, the narrowness, the drudgery and all the rest. I was free!

SLIGHTLY FOXED EDITIONS

No. 1 Rosemary Sutcliff, *Blue Remembered Hills*
No. 2 Diana Holman-Hunt, *My Grandmothers and I*
No. 3 V. S. Pritchett, *A Cab at the Door*
No. 4 Richard Kennedy, *A Boy at the Hogarth Press & A Parcel of Time*
No. 5 Priscilla Napier, *A Late Beginner*
No. 6 Adrian Bell, *Corduroy*
No. 7 Michael Wharton, *The Missing Will*
No. 8 James Lees-Milne, *Another Self*
No. 9 Ted Walker, *The High Path*
No. 10 Michael Jenkins, *A House in Flanders*
No. 11 Graham Greene, *A Sort of Life*
No. 12 Edward Ardizzone, *The Young Ardizzone*
No. 13 P. Y. Betts, *People Who Say Goodbye*
No. 14 Frances Wood, *Hand-grenade Practice in Peking*
No. 15 Ysenda Maxtone Graham, *Mr Tibbits's Catholic School*
No. 16 Dodie Smith, *Look Back with Love*
No. 17 Suzanne St Albans, *Mango and Mimosa*
No. 18 Elspeth Huxley, *The Flame Trees of Thika*
No. 19 Alan Moorehead, *A Late Education*
No. 20 Denis Constanduros, *My Grandfather & Father, Dear Father*
No. 21 Ysenda Maxtone Graham, *The Real Mrs Miniver*

Forthcoming

No. 23 Christabel Bielenberg, *The Past Is Myself*

Slightly Foxed Limited, 53 Hoxton Square, London N1 6PB
tel 020 7033 0258 · www.foxedquarterly.com